Mirrors
of His Glory

Mirrors of His Glory

Images of God from Scripture

John W. Sanderson

Presbyterian and Reformed Publishing Company
Phillipsburg, New Jersey

Unless otherwise noted, all Scripture quotations are from the HOLY BIBLE, NEW INTERNATIONAL VERSION. Copyright © 1973, 1978, 1984 International Bible Society. Used by permission of Zondervan Bible Publishers.

Copy editing by Edward W. Ojarovsky.
General editing and page design by Thom E. Notaro.
Manufactured in the United States of America.

Library of Congress Cataloging-in-Publication Data

Sanderson, John W.
    Mirrors of His glory : images of God from scripture / John W. Sanderson
        p.   cm.
    Includes bibliographical references and index.
    ISBN 0-87552-423-0
    1. God—Biblical teaching. 2. Bible—Language, style. 3. Bible—Devotional literature. I. Title.
BS544.S25 1991
231—dc20   90-42054

Contents

Preface

When Christians are asked, Who is God, and what is He like? the helpful answer from the *Westminster Shorter Catechism* may come to mind: "God is a Spirit, infinite, eternal, and unchangeable, in his being, wisdom, power, holiness, justice, goodness, and truth." Believers unfamiliar with the *Shorter Catechism* would probably still use many of the same words to speak of God. Such language drawn from Scripture expresses the character of God in literal terms.

The Bible also speaks about God in figurative terms, using figures of speech that vividly show us how God is like familiar things in the world He created. God said, for example, that He is like a father, a mother, a friend, a husband. We ought not be surprised that God likened Himself to human beings. After all, He created us in His image and after His likeness.

But God often compared Himself to other things in creation— both animate and inanimate—such as a bear or fire. Because He originally revealed Himself to people living in the Mediterranean basin, He used language that was a part of their ordinary lives. He called Himself a fountain, a rock, and a tower; a shepherd, a potter, and a vineyard keeper.

Such imagery is common in the Bible. And since God put it there, we must endeavor to understand its significance. We know that Bible study brings rich rewards, but those rewards come as a result of diligent work and total dependence on the Holy Spirit. No wonder Paul told Timothy, "Do your best to present yourself to God as one approved, a workman who does not need to be ashamed and who correctly handles the word of truth" (2 Tim. 2:15).

Figurative language in the Bible does not make the Bible an obscure book or mean that its great lessons are in doubt. A time-honored belief held by Christians is known as the perspicuity of the Bible. This doctrine is summarized in the *Westminster Confession of Faith:*

> All things in Scripture are not alike plain in themselves, nor alike clear to all: yet those things which are necessary to be known, believed, and observed for salvation, are so clearly propounded, and opened in some place of Scripture or other, that not only the learned, but the unlearned, in a due use of the ordinary means, may attain unto a sufficient understanding of them. (1.7)

Included in "the ordinary means" for gaining understanding of God's Word is the Bible itself. Scripture makes the claim that the more we know of the Word the better we will understand it. One of the purposes of the Book of Proverbs is "for understanding proverbs and parables, the sayings and riddles of the wise" (1:6). Moreover, the psalmist said, "The entrance of your words gives light; it gives understanding to the simple" (119:130). So a knowledge of the Bible can help us better understand the Bible.

In addition, the ministry of the Holy Spirit helps us understand the true meaning of God's revelation. We call this help "enlightenment." Paul told the Corinthians that "not many of you were wise by human standards." But because of the Spirit's word in their midst, they had "the mind of Christ" (1 Cor. 2:16).

In the pages that follow, we will study some of the more graphic images—both similes and metaphors—by which God has revealed Himself to His people. These "mirrors of His glory" generally reflect God at work in our world. With few exceptions, figures referring specifically to Jesus and the Holy Spirit have not been included. Most of the terms I have included originated in the Old Testament, but they are reaffirmed and confirmed by what we read in the New Testament. As the chapters are arranged, the imagery moves from personal relationships to inanimate objects, then to animals, and finally to occupations as symbols of God.

For study groups meeting on a 13-week schedule, chapters can be grouped into 13 lessons as follows:

Lesson	Chapters
1	Preface, 1
2	2, 3
3	4, 5, 6
4	7
5	8, 9
6	10, 11, 12
7	13, 14
8	15, 16
9	17
10	18, 19
11	20, 21
12	22, 23
13	24

It should be noted that the images contained herein were chosen, and much of the writing of this book was completed, prior to the publication of Richard Pratt's excellent work *Pray with Your Eyes Open*. In an appendix, Pratt lists many names, titles, and metaphors for God found in the Bible, and there is some overlapping between his selection and mine. I recommend his list for further study, as I highly commend his work itself.

Several standard theological works cited in the notes have been identified by the following abbreviations:

NICNT—The New International Commentary on the New Testament
NICOT—The New International Commentary on the Old Testament
TDOT—Theological Dictionary of the Old Testament
ZPED—The Zondervan Pictorial Encyclopedia of the Bible

Bibliographical information for these and other sources cited in the notes can be found in the reference list at the end of the book.

Although the bibliography will show how great a debt of gratitude I owe to many for help in looking into these mirrors of God's glory, I want to express thanks to those who were more immediately involved. My wife, Pearl, read the manuscript at every stage of its preparation and has made invaluable suggestions. Mrs. June Dare of Covenant Theological Seminary worked with great care and devotion in preparing the typescript. Mr. Keith Jones, a student at Covenant College, has prepared the Scripture index.

I am also grateful to Dr. Nicholas P. Barker, vice-president of Covenant College, and to Dr. David C. Jones, former dean of Covenant Seminary, for their many insightful suggestions. Although I have been dependent on them for guidance, they are in no way responsible for defects in the book. Thanks is due to friends at Presbyterian and Reformed Publishing Company for their careful scrutiny of the manuscript and for many suggestions for stylistic improvement.

Finally, I wish to thank God for enabling me to learn from and about Him. Of course that learning process still continues! I am beginning to appreciate Moses' words, "O Sovereign Lord, you have begun to show to your servant your greatness and your strong hand" (Deut. 3:24).

1. Word Games and God's Word

We don't know for certain how the ancient Israelites entertained themselves in their homes. But a good case can be made for their having played word games. The evidence suggests that many Israelites were experts at devising riddles, hard sayings, parables, and proverbs.

For instance, when Jotham wanted to rebuke the inhabitants of Shechem for murdering his 69 brothers and choosing Abimelech as their leader in Gideon's place (Judg. 9), he climbed nearby Mt. Gerizim and told a story. Shouting at length about olive trees, fig trees, and grape vines and then calling Abimelech a thorn bush, Jotham was telling the Shechemites that Abimelech could never provide them the protection they needed. Jotham's use of imagery made clear sense to his hearers, but they rejected his counsel and thus paid a price (v. 57).

Likewise, when Samson (Judg. 14) wanted to show his scorn for the men of Timnah for coercing his fiancee into revealing the meaning of his riddle to them, he told them another riddle. Its meaning must have been clear to them:

> If you had not plowed with my heifer,
>> you would not have solved my riddle.
>>> (v. 18)

And when Amaziah, king of Judah, wanted to pick a fight with the much stronger Jehoash, king of Israel (2 Kings 14), Jehoash tried to discourage him by speaking of thistles and wild beasts.

Such figurative language was not only used in the political arena, it also played a significant part in the messages the prophets brought to the people (cf. 2 Sam. 12:1-10; Ezek. 17; 19; 37). The use of vivid symbols and images was part of God's plan for making His Word known. When Miriam and Aaron opposed Moses in the wilderness because they thought he was taking too much upon himself, God rebuked them. In doing this He showed the difference between the way He would speak with Moses and the method He would use later with other prophets:

> When a prophet of the Lord is among you,
> I reveal myself to him in visions,
> I speak to him in dreams.
> But this is not true of my servant Moses;
>   he is faithful in all my house.
> With him I speak face to face,
>   clearly and not in riddles.
>
> (Num. 12:6-8)

God told Miriam and Aaron not only that Moses' place of leadership in Israel was due to divine arrangement but also that Moses would occupy a place of superiority even among the later prophets. This passage is important for what it says as well as for what it does not say. It says that God spoke to Moses in a very intimate way, literally "mouth to mouth" and "visibly" (v. 8). One might almost say that they spoke conversationally, as friends (cf. Exod. 33:11; Deut. 34:10). In contrast the prophets' messages would often come through visions and dreams, and sometimes consist in difficult statements requiring interpretation. This passage does give divine sanction to the use of figures in the Bible and indicates as well that they may require some study. The truth is, the Old Testament abounds in both literal and figurative statements, and both have been chosen as vehicles of God's truth.

The passage does not say, for example, that Isaiah's prophecy is less true than the Pentateuch, or that Jeremiah's writings are less certain of fulfillment than those of Moses. Note well that in the case of these later revelations God says, "I reveal myself . . . I speak" (v. 6). The passage does not say that figures of speech are lacking in Moses or that the prophets never use plainness of speech.

During His ministry Jesus often used figures of speech to press home a point. When approached by the Canaanite woman whose daughter was demon-possessed, He at first said nothing (Matt. 15:21ff.). He was not being heartless but was testing the depth of her faith. When she persisted, He answered, "I was sent only to the lost sheep of Israel." When she knelt at His feet, He replied, "It is not right to take the children's bread and toss it to their dogs." That sentence said more than could be explained in several paragraphs. But the woman's faith and perseverance was not to be denied. She said, "But even the dogs eat the crumbs that fall from their masters' table." Adopting the very metaphor used by the Master, she expanded on it with sincerity and intensity, and so her request was granted. Observing this exchange, the disciples learned a great lesson in faithful and importunate prayer.

The Benefits of Using Figures

The Bible is full of vivid metaphors and similes. They make it exciting to read but often difficult to understand. Why, then, does God use so many figures to describe Himself? There are a number of reasons. Let us consider some of the most important.

1. Focus of Attention

Oftentimes, something is right before our eyes, but we don't see it because our focus of attention is on something else.[1] For example, a moth in a clothes closet might escape our attention unless something (a hole in a garment) or someone alerts us to the need to look more closely. Similarly, we might not recognize that God is at work in the world because we are inattentive to how He works. But if we read in the Bible that sometimes God Himself acts like a moth, we might begin to look for quiet, unseen, and gradual effects of judgment being carried out by a sovereign God.

2. *Economy of Language*

Think how one word or a brief sentence can say more than a long paragraph. When some Pharisees told Jesus that He should leave Galilee because Herod Antipas wanted to kill Him, He replied,

> Go tell that fox, "I will drive out demons and heal people today and tomorrow, and on the third day I will reach my goal." (Luke 13:32)

By the use of one word, "fox," Jesus indicated that He had seen through the scheme of Herod. The king and the Pharisees were not friends, but they agreed in wanting Jesus out of Galilee. The Pharisees believed they could deal with Him more easily in Judea where they had more power. Antipas wanted him out of his territory because Jesus' message, like that of John the Baptist before Him, was an irritant he could not put up with. What better strategy could Herod devise than to have his enemies, the Pharisees, act as his messengers and urge Jesus to leave the region.

Perhaps Jesus also used the word *fox* (rather than, for example, *lion* or *eagle*, which were often symbols of royalty) to indicate His contempt for Herod as a ruler. A weak, pleasure-loving man, Herod was unable to stand up against such a popular figure as Jesus. Jesus showed His contempt by saying that He would continue His ministry in Galilee until it was finished. Then, and only then, would He leave Galilee for Judea and face the Pharisees there.

3. *Making the Unfamiliar Familiar*

In most languages, figures of speech help us to understand what would otherwise be strange. For example, the word *unchangeable* can cause us some difficulty because most of the things around us do change. How can I understand a being who is unchangeable? The Bible offers this helpful figure of speech:

> In the beginning you [God] laid the foundations of the earth,
>   and the heavens are the work of your hands.
> They will perish, but you remain;
>   they will all wear out like a garment.
> Like clothing you will change them
>   and they will be discarded.
> But you remain the same,
>   and your years will never end.
>   (Ps. 102:25ff.)

Here, the Bible tells us that God is not like the clothes we have that wear out and are discarded. We still do not comprehend God's eternity and unchangeableness, but we now grasp an essential part of the truth about Him, and we can put that truth into practice.

4. Making Some Things More Difficult

Unlike the reason given above, sometimes God used word images to make things difficult to accept for rebellious people who trifle with Him and His revelation. To do this, He often spoke in language that troubled and shocked.

Imagine yourself as an observing Jew in Jesus' day. For generations you and your ancestors had not drunk blood or eaten meat with blood in it. You did this out of faithfulness to God, who had forbidden it. To your utter amazement you hear Jesus saying, "... unless you eat the flesh of the Son of Man and drink his blood, you have no life in you" (John 6:53). Such graphic language caused a clear division within the disciples. Some said: "This is a hard teaching. Who can accept it?" And so they left and no longer followed Him. But Peter wanted to hear more: "Lord, to whom shall we go? You have the words of eternal life."

The overall effect was to make people who had been thinking superficially stop and consider the depth of their commitment. The merely curious were offended and left; they had no real interest in Jesus or His message. The true seekers became even more interested and so continued with the Master.

To His disciples Jesus gave the following explanation for speaking in this figurative way:

> The knowledge of the secrets of the kingdom of heaven has been given to you, but not to them. . . . This is why I speak to them in parables. (Matt. 13:11ff.)

He further explained that the popular reaction to His words was a fulfillment of Isaiah 6:9-10:

> "Be ever hearing, but never understanding;
>   be ever seeing, but never perceiving."
> Make the heart of this people calloused;
>   make their ears dull
>   and close their eyes.
> Otherwise they might see with their eyes,
>   hear with their ears,
>   understand with their hearts,
> and turn and be healed.

Jesus' message was not for the seeker of new doctrines for novelty's sake. It was, rather, for the one who allowed himself or herself to be disturbed by a new idea and whose interest was whetted to inquire further as to what these hard sayings might mean.

5. *"Feathers for Arrows"*

The phrase "feathers for arrows" is borrowed from the title of Spurgeon's book of sermon illustrations. It probably describes the use of figures more accurately than any other phrase. Some comparisons drive home a point far more effectively and make the truth far more vivid than even a good argument. And often even well-known thoughts are reinforced by a good illustration. To use words by J. I. Packer, "Listeners are nudged into seeing old facts in a new light."[2]

6. Clues to the Speaker's (or Writer's) State of Mind

Often, figures of speech give a clue to the way the speaker or writer is thinking. This is the viewpoint adopted by Lakoff and Johnson in *Metaphors We Live By*. For example, former Soviet Premier Krushchev on a memorable occasion spoke of "burying" the Western world. His figure of speech bespoke a state of mind committed to seeing history as an inexorable dialectic that would destroy all who oppose it. Further, evolutionists see life as an impersonal process in which only the "fit" survive.

How different are the figures of speech that express a view of life under the God of the Bible!

- He is potter, shaping human lives and their destinies.
- He is bookkeeper and judge, and someday He will grant true justice on the basis of what He knows.
- He is Lord, and He expects a return from His servants.
- He is water, giving life and refreshment to His creatures.
- He is mother, giving comfort and affection to those who delight in Him.

Understandably, the reader may be puzzled initially by the thought that the God who forbade images of Himself has used so many images to make Himself known. But there is a clear and important difference between the images forbidden in the Second Commandment and the imagery found in Scripture. God in essence told Israel, "I don't want *you* to make any image of Me because any such image, made out of your sinful imagination, will be misleading and a lie." If these visual images of God from our imagination teach us anything at all (as some claim they do), they inevitably teach error. But to help us truly know Him better, God has basically told us, "I am at work in the world in a way that resembles fire, water, a potter, or a moth. If you think of me for a moment as a rock or a friend, you will learn an important truth about Me. Only don't take something I have used to reveal Myself and make it a permanent image supposedly to help you worship Me." (In this connection, study Num. 21:4-9; 2 Kings 18:4; John 3:14f.).

Most of the figures of speech God has used to describe

Himself are commonplace expressions dealing with familiar ideas. But a particular image can produce in us a new and stirring experience, as we see the old truth in a new light. What had been ordinary or routine is suddenly seen as a provocative, nagging, even inconvenient, reality.

Notes

[1] See James Gleick's *Smithsonian* article, "New Images of Chaos," in which he quotes Robert Shaw, "You don't see something until you have the right metaphor to let you perceive it" (p. 128).

[2] Geisler, *Inerrancy*, 210.

Part One

Personal Relationships
as
Mirrors of His Glory

2. Father

As students in a seventh-grade vocational guidance class, we had spent the semester learning about many occupations that would be open to us later in life. There was also a near-term significance to the class, since our choice of an occupation would determine which high school we should attend and which courses we should choose in that school.

So we all made our choices. I remember that I wanted to be an astronomer. We were instructed to tell our parents about what we had decided and to bring back a note indicating their approval. For most of us it was all routine, but not for one boy who sat at a desk near me. His choice to become a lawyer brought a visit to the class from his father. Bursting into the room as we were getting organized for the day, the father told the teacher in front of us all that *his* son was to be no lawyer. *His* son would grow up to be a fruit vendor like himself! No school teacher was going to try to make his son into what the child could never be.

The teacher became nonplused, embarrassed, and upset all at once. For our part, we students enjoyed every moment of it. It wasn't often that our teacher was on the receiving end of a tirade!

Only on later reflection did I realize what had happened in

11

that confrontation. The teacher's authority had receded into the background as the concerned father had taken center stage. His actions may have been crude and ill-advised, but he had come across as a father whose first concern was for his son and his son's future. No one, not even a teacher, was going to point his son in a wrong direction. Rightly or wrongly (for I have long since lost track of my classmate), the father thought he knew his son and what he could and couldn't do. And he wanted to protect him from making a wrong choice.

The writer of Psalm 103 had had experiences similar to that of my classmate. Both his earthly father and his heavenly Father had shown understanding and compassion as they directed him on his pathway in life.

Psalm 103

Although the pagan nations surrounding Israel called their own god "father" with a variety of meanings, it is clear that the psalmist was speaking of the Lord as a father in a very specialized sense. He was not endorsing an indiscriminate "father of mankind." God is the father of those whom He has forgiven and redeemed (vv. 3-4). He has removed their transgressions and does not treat them as they deserve (vv. 10, 12).

God, like many fathers in Israel, has compassion on His children. The psalmist has already referred to this attribute of God in verse 8, where he alludes to Exodus 34:6, a much-quoted verse in the Old Testament. In that passage, God reveals Himself to Moses, at the latter's request, as compassionate and gracious, slow to anger and abounding in love and faithfulness. Compassion is the kind of love that often springs from a close personal relationship. The Hebrew word for "compassion" is closely associated with the word for "womb." On other occasions it is used for the feeling people have for the helpless and oppressed. It is close to "pity."

"For he knows how we are formed, he remembers that we are dust" (v. 14). Many acts of human compassion are based on ignorance or misinformation, and many are carried out in an ill-conceived way. The end is frustration or a miscarriage of the goodness intended. The psalmist tells us that this will not happen in God's gracious dealings with His children. He understands and knows best how to respond to us.

God Understands Us as Fallen Creatures

Genesis 2 tells us that God made Adam "from the dust of the ground." Originally this "dust" was not a token of weakness but a sign that human beings would be part of the physical creation and, indeed, stewards of it. Then He "breathed into his nostrils the breath of life." This meant that Adam also partook of a spiritual creation. Man received his life not by a command of God as the other animals did (cf. Gen. 1:20ff.), but by a special creative act of the Lord. We simply do not know what feats of strength and prowess unfallen human beings might have attained to. What we, alas, do know is that Adam and Eve chose disobedience to God, and they, and the race coming from them, have suffered the consequences ever since. These consequences, at least in part, are spelled out in the verses surrounding Psalm 103:13-14.

"He remembers that we are dust." "Dust" has now become a sign of weakness, of being fragile and short-lived like grass and the flower of the field. Like last month's cut flowers, which are cast away and forgotten, so is the power and glory of human beings. God remembers this, and perhaps this is the reason why He requires so little of His children. There are some, to be sure, who accomplish great things, but we can find comfort in Paul's reminder that God places a high value on faithfulness in little things (1 Cor. 4:2), which even the least of us is capable of.

Because God remembers we are dust His fatherly care is seen in His preventive providence. Many things do not happen to His children because God knows what the destructive consequences would be. "When Pharaoh let the people go, God did not lead them on the road through the Philistine country, though that was shorter. For God said, 'If they face war, they might change their minds and return to Egypt'" (Exod. 13:17). How many things have been kept out of our lives by an understanding God who knows that we are dust?

We should interpret Paul's "thorn in the flesh" in the same way (2 Cor. 12:7). Paul had received "surpassingly great revelations." He had led many people to Christ and had planted many churches in strategic areas. All of these things would turn the head of a man made of dust. So God gave his child a constant reminder of his weakness "to keep me from becoming conceited." How many things come into our lives by an understanding God who knows that we are dust?

For this same reason God "will not always accuse, nor will he harbor his anger for ever." These statements do not apply to everyone; they apply only to God's children who have been forgiven by Him. Because He knows that we are dust, He anticipates our sinning (though He never condones it). In the early days of Israel's existence as a nation, God made provision for the people's sins. In Leviticus 16, He told the high priest "to lay both hands on the head of the live goat [often called the "scapegoat"] and confess over it all the wickedness and rebellion of the Israelites—all their sins—and put them on the goat's head" (v. 21). This was to be done yearly because the Lord knew that His people would sin. It was a type and symbol of what Jesus the Messiah would do, once and for all, for those who would put their trust in Him. In view of that work of Christ and the provision He made, not only for the removal of sins but also for the reinstatement of the penitent, our Father promises not to harbor anger forever.

He Understands Us as Saints

Because of Christ, sinners become saints. This is the work of God just as truly as His original creation was. God understands the hopes and desires of His children and cares for them in view of that understanding.

Just as Adam and Eve were capable of obedience in the Garden of Eden, so God's renewed children "keep his covenant and remember to obey his precepts" (Ps. 103:18). But there is a difference. Our best obedience is mixed, in that it both proceeds from God's Spirit and is wrought by us. It can never earn us forgiveness or gain us "brownie points" before God. Nevertheless, God is pleased to accept and reward our good works even though they are accompanied by weakness and imperfection.[1]

We see this understanding attitude illustrated constantly in human affairs. Parents and, especially, grandparents delight in what children do, not because of the high quality of the work but because it is their children who do it. Whenever we ourselves express this attitude, as we see it manifested in others, we should be reminded of God's attitude toward His children. He is aware of their weaknesses but is pleased to accept and reward what is sincere, because He looks upon His children through the merits of His Son.

This gracious attitude applies not only to the weaknesses of His redeemed children but also to their renewed desires and aspirations: "He satisfies my desires with good things, so that my youth is renewed like the eagle's" (v. 4). Two extremes are to be avoided here. One mistake is to think that God has called us to "the good life" in a material sense so that Christians may live in luxury and pampered ease. To refute this idea one need only read some of Paul's statements, such as 1 Corinthians 4:11ff. or 2 Corinthians 4:7.

The other extreme is illustrated by a quote from a young boy: "Ice cream must be of the devil because it tastes so good"—as though enjoyment of any material blessing is denied to the people of God altogether.

Between these extremes lies the truth that God often encourages His saints by satisfying their desires and renewing their spirits. A look at verse 5 in various translations shows that it is difficult to translate, but the overall meaning of the verse is clear: our heavenly Father often grants our desires and frequently does much more than we ask. There is an interesting anecdote in 2 Samuel 23. While fighting the Philistines, David expressed a desire for water from a spring in Bethlehem, his boyhood home. He was the anointed king, and if he had been reigning, his wish might have been granted easily. As it was the Philistines blocked the way to Bethlehem and three of David's men had to risk their lives to obtain the water. God heard David's request and satisfied his passing desire, thus encouraging him to believe that he had not been forgotten. At the same time he gave added assurance that the time would come when David would not only have access to the well and its water, but would also rule the land.

Our desires will not always be met in such a spectacular way, but we should expect our Father to delight in us as much as earthly fathers delight to give their children what they ask for.

William Cowper has put all this in proper perspective.

> Sometimes a light surprises the Christian while he sings;
> It is the Lord, who rises with healing in his wings;
> When comforts are declining, He grants the soul again
> A season of clear shining, to cheer it after rain.

The entire hymn, along with the passages in Malachi 4 and Habakkuk 3 on which it is based, puts our needs and desires in proper perspective.

God's blessing His children in this way is not an end in itself. It results in refreshment in body and spirit: "My youth is renewed like the eagle's." Interpreters follow two leads here. First, youth is renewed in the same way as an eagle's youth is; this is usually understood as a reference to the legend that the eagle renews its youth by flying towards the sun and then diving into the sea. A second, and in my opinion more plausible, interpretation is that youth is restored so that one has the strength and vigor of an eagle. This understanding then parallels Isaiah 40:31:

> . . . those who hope in the Lord
>   will renew their strength.
> They will soar on wings like eagles;
>   they will run and not grow weary.

God has promised His children a spiritual "second wind" in both mind and body. We receive a fresh supply of fortitude and vigor for the providences of a new day. We enjoy each of these blessings, because God has chosen to be our Father and to love us as His children.

Proverbs 3:11-12

There is a balance in God's revelation to us. Just as He satisfies our desires with good things, so He also sends us difficulties of many kinds. As Paul wrote to the Philippians, "It has been granted to you on behalf of Christ not only to believe on him, but also to suffer for him" (1:29). Suffering has a variety of purposes, and one of them is discipline, or education.

The context of Proverbs 3 exhibits the balance we spoke of in the preceding paragraph:

- blessing for those who trust (vv. 5-6)
- health and success for those who fear and obey (vv. 7-8)
- prosperity for those who are generous (vv. 9-10)
- discipline for those he loves (vv. 11-12).

Delitzsch summarizes the section as follows: "As God should not be forgotten in days of prosperity, so one should not suffer himself to be estranged from Him by days of adversity."[2]

God has revealed several motives for disciplining us.

First, He *loves* His redeemed children, and so He is like a father who disciplines his children because he loves and delights in them. God does not compare Himself to just any father. Throughout Proverbs, the father and mother held up as examples to follow are covenant parents. Worldly parents may be unjust and cruel, but such people are not in the author's view here. God is like a covenant parent who has Scripture as the rule and a deep concern for true piety.

Seen in this light, God educates and disciplines not only by Scripture but also by His providence. Daily He orders our lives so that we become more holy. Note that His discipline is not to make us acceptable to society's mores but to make us holy. Unholiness and sorrow go together not only in this life but also in eternity. So also, holiness and happiness are conjoined. That is why God in love disciplines His children. He desires their happiness, and only holiness can bring that.

This explains why God sometimes seems at variance with our desires and our judgments. We want certain things to happen that we think are best for us, but God obviously thinks otherwise! *We* are interested in success or short-term happiness. *He* is much more interested in our holiness. The best case in point is Job's experience. A godly man, Job also wanted good health, social acceptance, and continued well-being. The Book of Job makes clear that God desired of Job even greater godliness and a fuller sense of His majesty before Job's other desires might be granted.

Second, God reveals His desire to discipline us because He wants us to be comforted as we endure chastening. When the writer to the Hebrews cited Proverbs 3:11-12, he did so with the following introduction: "You have forgotten that word of encouragement that addressed you as sons" (12:5). Surely when we understand the reason for some difficulty in our lives, we can endure it better. If we are persuaded that our suffering is unnecessary, we are likely to become bitter. But if our trials can be seen in a meaningful framework, we may even be grateful for them. So the writer tells us that hardship should be treated as evidence that we are children of God. God has brought it into our lives for good, and that good must be defined as sharing in His holiness, as experiencing a harvest of righteousness and peace. Therefore, he urges us to submit to God's discipline and be trained by it (cf. 12:7-11).

This sentiment has been expressed in a stanza of the hymn "More Love to Thee, O Christ."

> Let sorrow do its work, Send grief and pain;
> Sweet are thy messengers, Sweet their refrain,
> When they can sing with me, More love, O Christ to thee.
> More love to thee, more love to thee.

Malachi 1:6

Thus far in our study we have seen God use the figure of a father to describe His attitudes and actions toward His chosen children as He cares for, and educates, them. In Malachi's time God used the same figure to express His sorrow and moral outrage at the hypocrisy and complacency of those children He had brought back from exile.

The exile did not produce a lasting change in the hearts of the people of Judah. When the time came to return from Babylon to reconstitute themselves as the people of God, only a few chose the arduous task of reclaiming the city and the land. Whatever zeal they may have had at the beginning was soon lost, and the work lagged. Under prodding from Haggai and Zechariah, the temple was finished, but the people were much more interested in their own houses and affairs. Their enthusiasm was further tempered by their intermarriages with the local people whose religion at best was a mixture of pagan and Jewish elements.

So by Malachi's time the situation was intolerable. Those Jews returning were evidently religious; they worshiped at the temple, brought sacrifices, and observed some of the requirements of the law. But their hearts were not in any of it. God's service had become an intolerable burden (1:13). He was not worth a healthy animal, which after all might bring a good price at the market. The priests were no better. They did not enforce the standards God had set, nor did they follow them in their own lives (2:1ff.). What made matters even worse was that what they offered to God, the great King, they would not think of offering to the governor who had been set over them (1:8).

Malachi was sent to condemn these ungodly attitudes and the practices that grew from them. His message reminded the people of God's fatherly care for them as a nation, in stark contrast to the judgment He had brought on neighboring Edom (1:2-5). Malachi also urged upon them the fact that fatherhood has its privileges.

The law called Israel to filial piety (Exod. 20:12; Lev. 19:3; Prov. 30:11,17), and the breaking of that law brought the severest of penalties (Deut. 21:18ff.). So Malachi's words would carry added weight for a people who had been schooled in parental obedience.

The prophet was, in effect, accusing the people of offering God their second best. Doing one's second best can be an attractive idea. It gives the outward appearance of devotion, while inwardly it can soothe the conscience interested only in superficialities. But such an attitude can only coexist with the idea of a second-rate God—it is inconsistent with the idea of a holy God. Note the vehemence with which God rebukes the people and their priests: "I will accept no offering from your hands" (1:10), "I will spread on your faces the offal from your sacrifices" (2:3).

Yet the temptation to offer one's second best is ever with us. This was Cain's problem (Gen. 4:5-7), and the Laodiceans were plagued by it as well (Rev. 3:15-16). It may also have been Timothy's difficulty, for Paul was compelled to urge him "to fan into flame the gift of God" (2 Tim. 1:6) and to "endure hardship with us like a good soldier of Christ Jesus" (2:3). Was Timothy tempted to cowardice because of a fear of persecution? This may have tempered his zeal so that he was willing to do less than his best in the ministry in Ephesus. Whatever Timothy's situation might have been, a caring Father led the apostle to write the word of warning and encouragement.

John 20:17

Jesus was aware that "father" meant something quite different to Him than it meant to Mary of Magdala. He called God "Father" when He wanted to assert His own deity. He also called God the "Father" of believers when He wanted to assert that the Gospel brought them into the relationship with God that, we have seen, was part of the Old Testament revelation. Since both doctrines were essential parts of His message, the word *father* was often on His lips.

This fact is borne out by some statistics. Matthew speaks of God as "Father" 64 times; Mark, 18; Luke, 56; and John, 122. As we conclude this chapter, we are concerned with Jesus' revelation of God as the Father of believers.

Jesus stressed the fatherhood of God to protest against the legalism of His day. The Pharisees were devoted to a code of righteousness, not to a person. To them, piety was a matter of doing acts of righteousness in public. So when they gave to the needy, they announced it with trumpets; when they prayed, they did so on street corners; when they fasted, they disfigured their faces to show people they were fasting. To be holy in that fashion took much time and much money. Pharisees had a lot of time and money, but the common people were short of both. Hence, the latter weren't considered pious and were made to bear a great sense of guilt.

Confronted with that frame of mind, Jesus talked not about observing a code of piety but of a Father who cared much more about the heart than He did about the outward appearance. This teaching of Jesus was not something new (cf. 1 Sam. 16:7), but under the Pharisees' tutelage it had been forgotten. And so it came as a new emphasis from the lips of Jesus. How strange His teaching must have sounded to the common people when He recited the Beatitudes:

> Blessed are the poor in spirit [but we have been taught that only the big givers will be blessed]. . . .
> Blessed are those who hunger and thirst for righteousness [but our teachers say that "righteousness" means outward acts]. . . .
> Blessed are the merciful [but deeds of mercy cannot be done on the Sabbath and should never be done for our enemies]. . . .

Jesus did not quarrel with the Pharisees in their devotion to the law (cf. Matt. 23:3, 23), but He insisted on a new orientation. The Law-giver should not be forgotten in the midst of law-keeping, and this was the Pharisees' error. The Law-giver was the Savior of Israel who had brought them out of Egypt, out of the land of slavery. He was a Father who was compassionate and merciful, because He understood the children He had made and had delivered from sin. And He was concerned with their hearts first and only secondly with their outward conduct.

As He did so frequently, Jesus brought an old, old message that seemed new because it had been forgotten and then superseded by the tradition of the elders. As He honored His Father, so He wants earthly children to respond to their heavenly Father with affection and devotion.

Notes
[1] The language of this paragraph is taken from the Westminster Confession of Faith, chap. 16.
[2] Keil and Delitzsch, *Biblical Commentary on the Proverbs of Solomon,* 1:90.

3. Mother

As a boy I learned early that my father, who was a physician, knew how to treat skinned knees. He would paint on the wound antiseptics, which would sting, burn, and generally cause a youngster pain. My cuts always healed, and I never developed an infection on the area he treated.

I also discovered that my mother had a way of treating skinned knees that seemed just as effective but did not produce pain of any sort. She would kiss the injured area, tell me that it was "all better," and send me out to play again. Although this may cause an outcry from the medical profession, I can testify that I never developed an infection on the area she kissed. Other mothers, I have discovered, produce that same sort of "cure" for their children. It is a gift from God, and we are all the better for it.

Several times in Isaiah's prophecies, God used the figure of a mother to describe His future dealings with Israel. Sometimes He called Jerusalem "mother." He likened the city to a barren woman who would have children sometime in the future (54:1-10) and to a mother whose children had forsaken her, though God would later restore them (51:17-23).

On two occasions God likened Himself to a mother as He predicted future blessings to the children of Abraham, who, because of their sins, suffered so grievously during the exile. We will study a passage later where both God and Jerusalem are likened to a mother.

Isaiah 49:15

The people of Judah had accused God of forgetting them (v. 14). On the surface they had good reason to think so. After all, they had suffered during the last days of Judah's existence. Faced by the might of Babylon, they had appealed to Egypt for protection, but to no avail. Then came the terrible siege so vividly portrayed by the prophet in the Book of Lamentations. Those not slain were taken captive and were living as displaced persons in Babylon, and there was no obvious evidence that the Babylonians would ever let them return to their homeland.

The emotions of discouragement, cynicism, and hopelessness set in. Whatever comfort the exiles could receive from the existing prophecies—words of restoration and future blessing— was dispelled by the harsh realities of their present existence. God must have forgotten!

In this situation God likened Himself to a mother. Could she ever forget her children? Could she ever withhold compassion from them? One is reminded of the prostitute's reaction when Solomon proposed splitting her baby in two so that both she and her neighbor might at least have half a child. How like a true mother she acted: "Please, my lord, give her the living baby! Don't kill him." By this proposal Solomon determined who the true mother was and awarded the child to her (1 Kings 3:16ff.).

Of course, in this sinful world a small minority of mothers might not act with such concern. Allowing for that possibility, God insists, "Though she may forget, I will not forget you" (v. 15). To underscore the impossibility of His forgetting them, He speaks of having engraved His children on His hands, of having the walls of Jerusalem before His eyes.

Because of God's faithfulness, great things would happen in the future. Jerusalem's sons and daughters would return to the city, borne and protected by the same Gentiles who had been persecuting them. The Jews would say, "This place is too small for us; give us more space to live in" (v. 20).

The Bible gives us many commands to "remember": we remember the Sabbath and we remember Christ's death. But an even greater revelation is that our Lord remembers.

Remember is a very significant word in Scripture, and its meaning must be clearly understood. When we use the word, we sometimes mean that we recall something we have forgotten, that we recollect something we have not thought of for a while. Obviously, this meaning of the word cannot be applied to God. He is omniscient: "Nothing in all creation is hidden from God's sight. Everything is uncovered and laid bare before the eyes of him to whom we must give account" (Heb. 4:13).

But other meanings of the word apply to Him as well. Some of these are "take to heart," "consider," "dwell on." These definitions indicate a mental activity, of course, but they also suggest an act of the will and often express great emotion. The Lord said concerning Israel, "Is not Ephraim my dear son, the child in whom I delight? Though I often speak against him, I still remember him. Therefore my heart yearns for him; I have great compassion for him" (Jer. 31:20). Jeremiah prayed concerning himself, "You understand, O Lord; remember me and care for me" (15:15). The psalmist confidently wrote, "The Lord remembers us and will bless us" (115:12). Contrariwise, Jeremiah warned a disobedient people, "He will now remember their wickedness and punish them for their sins" (14:10). In other words, when God "remembers," He takes action—in blessing or judgment.

We should be encouraged that God remembers our prayers, for example, those of Rachel and Hannah for children (Gen. 30:22; 1 Sam. 1:11, 19). Samson asked to be remembered, and he received his strength again (Judg. 16:28).

The Lord especially honors His covenant promises and His oath (Gen. 8:1; Exod. 2:24). The books of the Kings show God's faithfulness to the Davidic covenant when He preserved David's dynasty, even though several wicked kings led the nation astray (cf. 1 Kings 11:12f., 32-39; 15:4; 2 Kings 8:19; 19:34; 20:6). As

Edward Mote has written in the hymn "My Hope Is Built":

> His oath, his covenant, his blood
> Support me in the whelming flood;
> When all around my soul gives way,
> He then is all my hope and stay.

When God remembers, certain of His attributes come to the fore. The psalmist celebrated His love and faithfulness when he thought of the fact that nations outside Israel would hear the message of salvation (98:3). Zechariah was reminded of God's mercy when he realized that the Messiah had been born (Luke 1:72, 78).

It also happens that when God remembers works of evil, He acts because of the sanctity of His name (compare Ps. 74:18-23). And He blesses His covenant people, despite their sins, only for the sake of His holy name (Isa. 43:25; Jer. 14:21).

To summarize, when a child of God is tempted to think he or she has been forgotten by God, that temptation should be rejected by recalling what He has promised. He will remember His name, His covenant, His mercy and truth. He will recall our plight and our prayers.

As we have noted above, God's remembrance is not a passing thing: "I have engraved you on the palms of my hands" (Isa. 49:16). As Delitzsch wrote: "The picture of Zion (not merely the name, as ver. 16b clearly shows) is drawn in the inside of Jehovah's hands, just as men are accustomed to burn or puncture ornamental figures [today we would call them tatooes] and mementoes upon the hand, the arm, and the forehead. . . . There is the figure of Zion, unapproachable to every creature, as close to Him as He is to Himself, and facing Him amidst all the emotions of His divine life."[1]

God's remembering as a mother well prepares us to consider next His comforting as a mother.

Isaiah 66:13

I recall one of the more vicious slurs we children used to make: "He [or she] has a face only a mother could love." Though not a compliment to the ones spoken of, it certainly was a compliment to their mothers.

Something of this sentiment applies to God's love for sinners, and it expresses the kind of comfort God promised to His ancient people. As we said, they had become exiles because of their sins, and the exile had done little to make the majority of them penitent. Their lives were continually made miserable when their captors made fun of them, demanding songs of joy. "Sing us one of the songs of Zion" (Ps. 137:3). As the prophets predicted, the people of God had become "a hissing and a byword among the nations." Erstwhile friendly nations turned against them (Lam. 1:19; Obad. 10ff.).

But while earth offered them no present comfort or the promise of future comfort, God's message through Isaiah promised a strong consolation: "As a mother comforts her child, so will I comfort you; and you will be comforted over Jerusalem." The message of Isaiah 66 is somewhat complicated by the fact that first Jerusalem, then the Lord, are pictured as mothers. It will be helpful to look at the whole chapter in order to clear this up.

Verses 1-4. Israel as a whole is rebuked for thinking that hypocritical worship would be acceptable to God. The people think that having the temple in their midst, with its various sacrifices, automatically guaranteed God's blessing. So their worship had become indifferent and without godly feeling. Therefore God will choose harsh treatment for them.

Verses 5-6. But a godly remnant still trembles at His Word. They will escape judgment as they witness God's judgment on His enemies.

Verses 7-9. God will use them to repopulate the city. "A nation will be born in a day."

Verses 10-12. The children who now populate Zion will be nursed by a renewed Jerusalem. As a mother, Jerusalem will nurse them, carry them on her arm, and dandle them on her knees.

Verse 13. Jerusalem is not the source of their comfort but only the channel. Indeed, God is the source of this mother-love and will comfort them in Jerusalem.

From Isaiah's perspective, the restoration of Jerusalem would begin with the return from exile; from ours, it continues on into the New Testament (compare Gal. 4:26) and ultimately into the eternal state (Rev. 21:2).

We must now examine this twofold mother figure. First, Jerusalem as mother, then the Lord as mother.

The comfort God promised through Jerusalem is what most of us have received from our mothers: we have been "nursed," "carried," and "dandled." The first two verbs describe total care and intimacy. There will be no unsatisfied need, no sense of being forgotten, and no sorrow, for the present blessings will cause the past sins and sorrows to be forgotten.

The third verb, "dandled," shows the keen delight God will have for His children. This is expressed by the Hebrew word *hephzibah*, "my delight is in her" (62:4), and by Zephaniah's message: "He will take great delight in you, he will quiet you with his love, he will rejoice over you with singing" (3:17). Above all, it is the promise of the Aaronic benediction: "the Lord make his face shine upon you and be gracious to you; the Lord turn his face toward you and give you peace" (Num. 6:25). When we set alongside each other the pitiable state of the exiles and the delight God took in them, we have a fresh understanding of His amazing grace.

The idea that God delights in us is often difficult to believe and to act upon. We more easily believe that He is only a stern judge or, at best, a tolerant disciplinarian. Our understanding of the truth, however, depends on our acceptance of what the Bible calls "imputation." How can God delight in us? In the first place, because He has imputed our sins to another (Isa. 53:6), and He does not impute our sins to us (Ps. 32:2). Secondly, He does impute Jesus' righteousness to us, and we are accepted in Him (Rom. 5:19). Unless we take this imputation seriously, we shall never know that God delights in us.

This comfort, which comes from our confidence in the imputation of Christ's righteousness, also brings His peace and untold prosperity: "I will extend peace to her like a river, and the wealth of nations like a flooding stream" (v. 12). This peace comes with the righteousness mentioned in the paragraph above. But Isaiah tells us twice in this section of his prophecy, "There is no peace for the wicked" (cf. 48:22; 57:21).

Underlying this twofold figure of mother is the truth the New Testament makes more explicit. "Jerusalem" is not the city of buildings and walls but the fellowship of the remnant, "a dwelling in which God lives by his Spirit" (Eph. 2:22). As the citizens of the renewed city take their place and use their gifts, each individual is ministered to and receives the comfort of being a part of that fellowship.

We see this comforting fellowship at work in a number of New Testament passages. Onesiphorus often refreshed Paul, especially in Rome, where he searched hard to find the apostle. Prior to that time, he had helped Paul in many ways in Ephesus (2 Tim. 1:16ff.). Philemon had done the same thing for saints in Colosse, and Paul hoped that he would do the same for him by obeying the apostolic letter (Philem. 7, 20). Certainly, the Philippians comforted Paul when he was in prison by the gift Epaphroditus had brought from them (4:14ff.). Paul himself had been a comforting mother among the Thessalonians, caring for them as little children, when they had first come to Christ (1 Thess. 2:7).

We are not told explicitly how these saints refreshed one another, but we may infer that their acts included hospitality, companionship, and gifts of money. Encouragement also came when one saint could see the fruit of the Spirit in evidence in the conduct of another.

Thus it becomes clear that while David could say, "He [the Lord] restores my soul," He frequently does so through the saints. And this truth is at the heart of Isaiah's message.

When a mother kisses a skinned knee and pronounces it "all better," we forget the pain and run off to play again. Similarly, God's comfort brings His children forgetfulness of sorrow.

Notes
[1] Keil and Delitzsch, *Biblical Commentary on the Prophecies of Isaiah*, 2:269.

4. Brother

One day Tom Sawyer went out of the house, and the first person he met was the new boy on the street. The boys immediately took a dislike to each other, and an argument followed as to who could "lick" the other. After several side arguments and awkward pauses during which the antagonists tried to think of new ways to belittle the other, they started shoving each other. They struggled till they were hot and flushed. Then Tom said, "You're a coward and a pup. I'll tell my big brother on you, and he can lam you with his little finger, and I'll make him do it, too."

The new boy responded, "What do I care for your big brother? I've got a brother that's bigger than he is; and what's more, he can throw him over that fence, too."

At which point Mark Twain added parenthetically, "Both brothers were imaginary."

Imaginary or not, it is comforting to have a big brother who could take a smaller sibling's part and beat up all the opposition. Not all of us have had big brothers, and some who have, have found them wanting in the struggle for sibling supremacy. But the Bible promises that those who put their trust in Jesus Christ have an elder brother who can and will defend us against all His and our enemies.

We are introduced to Jesus as our brother in the Epistle to the

29

Hebrews. The letter was addressed to people who, because of persecution, were being tempted to abandon Jesus as their Savior and His church as a meeting place. How would you feel if as a Christian shopkeeper you were boycotted, or if as a Christian student you were harassed in school and had no friends, or if you found yourself being snubbed as a Christian and no one asked you to social events anymore? The temptation would be strong to question whether you had done the right thing by embracing Jesus as the Messiah and by no longer frequenting the synagogue. One of the arguments the writer uséd to guard Hebrew Christians against this temptation was that He is too close a relative and too wonderful a person for them to leave. The writer developed his reasoning along two lines: (1) Christ is a member of our family (the human race), and (2) He knows all about what it is to be human.

What the Bible teaches us about Jesus Christ remains a deep mystery, but two things are clear: Jesus is God, and He became a human being. The latter point is made in Hebrews 2:11ff.: Jesus ("who makes men holy") and His followers ("those who are made holy") are of the same family. He "shared in their humanity."

For this reason Jesus "is not ashamed to call them brothers." Our author quoted Psalm 22:22 as evidence for this statement. This quotation is very interesting because it came in the middle of a psalm that, in its first part, depicted the sufferings and death of the Messiah, and in the second part, described the worldwide effects of Messiah's work. Declaring God's name to His brethren was one of the first acts of the triumphant Messiah, and this indicated that He remains human even after His death and resurrection. The now-ascended Messiah, whom the Hebrews were being tempted to desert, was at that very moment acting as a high priest in heaven. In that capacity He was able to help the Hebrews with their problems, because as a human He had shared in them. As a human being He deliberately chose to have experiences like theirs and ours.

A few years ago I was hospitalized, along with eight or ten others, for treatment of diabetes. One of the members of our group faithfully followed the routine set for us by the physicians (eating a sugar-free diet, weighing the food before we ate it, and testing our blood for sugar levels). He even took a treadmill test to determine his heart condition. I was, therefore, surprised one day when he told me that he was not a diabetic. He was a male nurse, planning to specialize in diabetes treatment, and he wanted to have some idea of what his patients would be going through. Of course, he did not inject insulin, but in every other experience common to diabetics he was deliberately exposed to the regimen they followed. This is an example of what Jesus the Messiah did in the days of His flesh. "He had to be made like his brothers in every way."

The words "in every way" are important. They indicate that Jesus was tempted, just as we are, to have other gods, to make graven images, to misuse the name of the Lord, to desecrate the Sabbath, to dishonor His parents, to murder, to commit adultery, to steal, to give false testimony, and to covet. How many times was He tempted to be discouraged, bitter, and impatient?

So when you are suffering for your new-found faith and are a little bewildered by external pressures, what better helper can there be than someone who has also gone through the very same experiences? What better helper than someone who, because of kinship, is concerned for you? And what better helper than someone who has been elevated to power and is, therefore, in a place where He can really be of help?

He Does for Us What We Cannot Do

Many of us have such a superficial view of God that we do not realize what an impossible task it is for us sinners to please Him. The Israelites who were with Joshua at Shechem had experienced God's power and protection during their conquest of Canaan (Josh. 24). They thought the task of "mopping up" the land would be easy. And they took lightly the call Joshua had laid before them of serving the Lord amidst the idolatry that still persisted in the land. So they responded, "We too will serve the Lord, because he is our God" (v. 18).

Joshua was too acute a student of human nature to be taken

in by their statement. He knew that some people were willing to agree to anything when eager to get started in a new adventure. So he responded in a way some modern counselors might object to. Rejecting their superficial understanding of what lay ahead of them, Joshua told the Israelites:

> You are not able to serve the Lord. He is a holy God; he is a jealous God. He will not forgive your rebellion and your sins. (v. 19)

We misunderstand Joshua if we think he was trying to discourage his people. He was trying to turn them from their superficiality, so that they could soberly and realistically plan for their future and the future of their children. If they had listened to his words, they would have called upon God for His help in defending them from His and their enemies as they proceeded to keep His covenant in the land. As it turned out, "After that whole generation had been gathered to their fathers, another generation grew up, who knew neither the Lord nor what he had done for Israel" (Judg. 2:10).

One of the keys to success in most things in life is to learn what we cannot do, so that we can seek help when we need it. Joshua told the people that they could not serve God, and this lesson needs to be enforced today. "We know that whatever the law says, it says to them who are under the law, so that every mouth may be silenced and the whole world held accountable to God"[1] (Rom. 3:19). In our accountability to God, as well as in many other things, we need the help of an older brother.

In the second chapter of Hebrews the writer discusses how Jesus, our older brother, helps us in what we cannot do, as we shall now see.

He Is the Author of Our Salvation

As we saw above, salvation from sin is impossible by our own efforts. Not only is the debt too great, there is also the problem of our will: "No one seeks God" (Rom. 3:11). But Jesus not only had the will, He also had the ability. He became a human being and in His body made atonement for the sins of the people (Heb. 2:17). The footnote to verse 17 in the NIV gives what I believe is the correct interpretation of this verse: "and that he might turn aside God's wrath, taking away the sins of the people."

We often call this teaching the "substitutionary atonement," and that is a good way to express it. Jesus became our substitute. And when He died in our place, He bore the wrath of God for us, thus turning it away from us. Our sins were accounted His, and His death was reckoned ours. When the penalty was thus paid, our sins were taken away.

But it is a mistake to say that this is all there is to salvation. *Salvation* is a much more inclusive word, and the writer to Hebrews mentions one other truth that should be included in salvation: "he makes men holy" (v. 11). Of course, we become holy when Jesus' holiness is imputed to us. But it is equally true that we are becoming holy in a daily process in which we are renewed after the image of God in every part of our being, and the Holy Spirit enables us more and more to die to sin and to live to righteousness.

It is just here that an important practical point should be raised. How many times are we working at cross-purposes with God? It is natural for us to be interested in our own success, freedom, influence, and happiness. But God is more interested in our sanctification, in our being holy. So His daily providences, which are calculated to make us holy, may, and often do, produce situations that do not lead to our success, freedom, influence, or even happiness. Here the Christian often realizes that he or she has already made a commitment. God's way is best, and we accept it even when it runs counter to our plans. In the words of the hymn "More Love to Thee":

Once earthly joy I craved, Sought peace and rest;
Now thee alone I seek; Give what is best:
This all my prayer shall be, More love, O Christ, to thee.

Let sorrow do its work, Send grief and pain;
Sweet are thy messengers, Sweet their refrain,
When they can sing with me, More love, O Christ, to thee.

We can accept such providences because they are arranged by "a merciful and faithful high priest," who has been made like us in every way.

He Has Destroyed Satan

If we follow through with the biblical metaphor of Christ as the older brother who protects His younger siblings, then Satan takes on the character of a bully. This is not an inappropriate description. Though he is far from being God, Satan has power and wisdom far greater than human beings and uses them only for evil. Look at some of the ways the Bible describes him: "the ancient serpent called the devil or Satan, who leads the whole world astray . . . the accuser of our brothers, who accuses them before our God day and night" (Rev. 12:9-10); "Your enemy the devil prowls around like a roaring lion" (1 Pet. 5:8); "a liar and the father of lies" (John 8:44).

Our passage in Hebrews says that Jesus shared in our humanity "so that by his death he might destroy him who holds the power of death—that is, the devil." Two questions arise here. How did Jesus' death destroy Satan, and how does, or did, Satan hold the power of death? Let us discuss these in the reverse order.

The right to judge the world at the end of the age is the right of the Son of Man. He holds the keys of death and hell (cf. John 5:22; Rev. 1:18). How then can Satan have "the power of death"? "The whole [present] world is under the control of the evil one" (1 John 5:19), and the citizens and inhabitants of this world have no expectation but that of death. They follow "the ways of this world and of the ruler of the kingdom of the air, the spirit who is now at work in those who are disobedient" (Eph. 2:2). As long as they are under Satan's power, the people are subject to the sentence of death—and this is what the author of Hebrews seems to be saying.

Satan rules a kingdom, and it is a powerful one. He has ways of protecting his citizens from attacks from without and of satisfying their needs and desires so they are content to stay with him. But the gates of hell will not be able to withstand attack once Satan has been destroyed. This brings us to the first question: how did Jesus destroy him?

On the cross Jesus entered into Satan's kingdom and placed Himself under the power of death. He really died, and those who buried Him placed a corpse in the tomb. Jesus' resurrection was not only a display of divine power but also a victory over Satan, sin, and the grave. "He was raised to life for our justification" (Rom. 4:25). Jesus did not defeat Satan by brute force, as it were, but by the authority of God who found His sacrifice for sin acceptable, His death a proper substitution. What better display of that righteousness but to raise Him from the dead! Satan then no longer had the power over Him or over those who would put their trust in Him, the elect. Jesus could now enter the strong man's house and carry off his possessions because He had first tied up the strong man (cf. Matt. 12:29).

Although the final destination of Satan awaits Christ's second advent, it is a foregone conclusion. Christ and His younger siblings know that Satan is a defeated foe, and they can face up to his attacks. The bully may continue to bluster and threaten, but one greater than he, who shares in our humanity, has broken Satan's power.

He Helps Those Who Are Tempted

The help of Jesus comes in the first instance from the fact that He also is a human being. Having lived on earth as a human being and having deliberately undergone experiences common to all of us, Jesus as the high priest in heaven is able to help us. His is not theoretical knowledge. His experiences of success, sorrow, temptation, and weakness were not instances of play-acting. Jesus endured every temptation that can come to us, and He did not sin against His Father in the process. So the help He offers in time of need is the help of an expert—a veteran of many battles with Satan and temptation.

This theme of help is a recurring one in the epistle (cf. Heb. 4:14-16; 7:25; 10:19ff.). When we pray, help comes to us from the throne of grace where Jesus is now seated. Sometimes we hear people say in a moment of real need, "If only Jesus were here!" One answer to that remark is to point out that Jesus is now in the best possible place to help us. He can do more as our intercessor in heaven than He could do here on earth. The writer makes this point in 6:18-20. He uses an anchor to illustrate the hope we have in a now invisible Savior. An anchor does no good when it remains in the boat. An anchor works only when cast into the sea. But when that happens, the anchor can't be seen anymore! And that is why our hope in Jesus is like an anchor. He has disappeared into heaven. He is now at the mercy seat and cannot be seen. But like the invisible anchor, He is able to perform His work of helping us in time of need and even, thereby, to save us to the uttermost.

Because Jesus has become like us in every way, we may be sure His help will be effective. Moreover, we may be sure He will be patient with us; for although He did not succumb to any temptations, He understands their force. And He bears with us in the times when we fall.

The message to the sorely tempted Hebrews is twofold. Jesus as God is exalted far above the heavens. Therefore, He should be worshiped and served. Jesus as the God-Man understands our need and is not ashamed to call us brothers and sisters. So, count on His help when you need it.

Notes
[1] Hendriksen argues correctly, in my opinion, that the translation should be, ". . . it speaks to those (who are) within the pale of the law. . . ." Thus, the verse refers to the whole world (*Romans*, 124).

5. Friend

How do you react when you hear the comment "He (or she) hasn't a friend in the world"? It probably makes you think of someone lonely, pitiable, and wretched. Imagine—no one to talk to, no one with whom to share a secret, no one to help when you need it.

David might have found himself friendless. He was not especially beloved by his brothers or well-thought of by his father. He was hated by his new master, Saul, and a stranger in the king's court. But God gave David a true friend just when he needed him most. Jonathan does not usually rank high among the great in the Bible, but without him and his friendship David might never have been king. Jonathan loved David as himself (1 Sam. 18:3); and when he was killed, David said, "I grieve for you, Jonathan my brother; you were very dear to me. Your love for me was wonderful, more wonderful than that of women" (2 Sam. 1:26).

Just because friends are so close, some people have difficulty with calling God "friend." But this term has never been a problem with hymn writers. Study any hymnal containing the great hymns of the church and you will find many references to God as "friend."

Where did so many writers from different times and places

get the idea that God was their friend, and they were His? It all began, as so many truths of the Bible do, with Abraham. In his great prayer for help when Moab and Ammon were attacking him, Jehoshaphat prayed to God, "O our God, did you not drive out the inhabitants of this land before our people Israel and give it forever to the descendants of Abraham your friend" (2 Chron. 20:7). When God wished to encourage the exiles that He would again be merciful to them, He said, "O Israel, my servant, Jacob, whom I have chosen, you descendants of Abraham my friend" (Isa. 41:8). When James wanted to remind his readers that faith without works was dead, he pointed to Abraham who "'believed God, and it was credited to him as righteousness,' and he was called God's friend "(2:23).

But it is Jesus, in John 15, who gives the clearest revelation of the friendship between God and His redeemed people. Some would restrict what is said here to the band of disciples alone, but there is nothing in this section that must be understood solely of them. What He said here applies to all believers.

In describing our friendship with the Father, Jesus first revealed how it began. This friendship began with His choice, not ours (v. 16). Paul constantly stressed the doctrines of grace that trace all our blessings back to our election (Eph. 1:3). Our salvation is not of our initiative; it is not something that came as an afterthought on God's part. "I have loved you with an everlasting love; I have drawn you with loving-kindness" (Jer. 31:3). Our thinking about our salvation should focus on election much more than it commonly does. In an evening service years ago the leader paused to ask various members of the congregation how long they had been saved. Some said ten years; others, fifty. Soon a young man stood to say, "I have been waiting for someone to speak who has been saved as long as I have, because I am one of those who have been saved from before the foundation of the world." There was laughter, of course, but the young man had an important point. Our relationship with our Friend is an eternal one and will last into eternity future.

But it took an historical event to make our friendship with God a reality. "Greater love has no one than this, that one lay down his life for his friends" (v. 13). This is no armchair proverb but an accurate description of Jesus' entire earthly life. There can be no mutual interest between God and humans if there is still a rift caused by sin. Jesus removed that alienation when He gave His life for us and we were reconciled to God. We must understand that Christianity is a religion based on history. And when certain historical facts are denied or made into myths, the very heart of the Gospel is thereby destroyed.

In the passage before us, Jesus shows that God has proved His friendship to us in two important ways.

He Has Shared His Secrets with Us (John 15:15)

Jesus said that He has told us everything the Father told Him. Once again, we are brought face to face with the mystery of the incarnation. Jesus as God knows everything, but in His self-effacement He was dependent on His Father for knowledge and power. At any rate, Jesus told His friends, the disciples, whatever the Father had told Him. This fact is illustrated in the life of Abraham. When God appeared to him (Gen. 18), He asked the rhetorical question, "Shall I hide from Abraham what I am about to do?" Then He proceeded to tell His friend about His determination to destroy Sodom where Lot and his family were.

This is one way to read the Bible—as a letter from a friend who is sharing his secrets with us. When the Bible is read this way, it becomes an exciting book indeed.

In His friendship with us, God not only has told us His secrets but has also provided us with all we need for life and godliness (cf. 2 Pet. 1:3). God is not stingy with His blessings but with Christ has graciously given us all things.

He Answers Our Prayers (John 15:16b)

Again, an incident in the life of Abraham, God's friend, will illustrate what Jesus is promising us. Abraham's response to the word that Sodom would be destroyed was eloquent intercessory prayer (Gen. 18:23-33). There is no immediate indication that

God would answer that prayer, but Abraham evidently expected some response (cf. 19:27). The words of the angel in Genesis 19:21-22 make it clear that God had committed Himself to His friend. Lot was wavering in his desire to leave the city before it was destroyed, and he was unwilling to give full obedience to God. Instead of fleeing to the mountains for safety, he asked to be allowed to find refuge in Zoar, a small town nearby. The angel said:

> Very well, I will grant this request too; I will not overthrow the town you speak of. But flee there quickly, because I *cannot do anything* until you reach it. (emphasis added)

We are not accustomed to hearing God say "I can't." However when He binds Himself to His friend, God honors His promise. The disciples of Jesus can expect no less: "Then the Father will give you whatever you ask in my name" (John 15:16).

But friendships have two sides. Jesus tells us that in response to God's many acts of friendship, there is one obligation that He lays upon us: obedience.

> If you obey my commands, you will remain in my love, just as I have obeyed my Father's commands and remain in his love. (v. 10)

> You are my friends if you do what I command. (v. 14)

> You did not choose me, but I chose you to go and bear fruit—fruit that will last. (v. 16a)

Once again the life of Abraham will give us an illustration of his friendship with God. Compare Hebrews 11:8-19 with the events of Genesis 12 and 22. Abraham's was not a blind faith, although compared with what believers know today it was not very explicit. But Abraham knew God, that knowledge led him to trust, and that trust issued in obedience. His obedience is a challenge to all believers who have the full Bible as their guide.

True, Jesus is not requiring obedience as the way to blessing. But He is saying that since we have been so blessed as to be called God's friends, we should give the obedience God desires.

Just as human friendships do not just happen but are culti-
vated, so we must work at the new relationship we have with
God. At the end of this chapter we have listed some of the hymns
that celebrate God's friendship with us. When these hymns are
on our lips and in our hearts, we are encouraged to contemplate
that friendship.

But there are other ways to develop friendship. We should
meditate on the things Jesus has stressed in John 15.

First, we should daily thank Him for His sacrifice that made
our friendship possible. The stress is on the word *daily*. In the
tabernacle, priests were directed to offer a continuous burnt
offering. Each morning and each evening they sacrificed a bull
and laid it on the altar so that there was never a time when such
a sacrifice was not burning. This sacrifice was a worship offering
stressing praise and thanks to God for His mercy. It was "an
aroma pleasing to the Lord" (Lev. 1:17). We are reminded in
Romans 12:1-2 that the counterpart of the burnt offering is the
living sacrifice the believer offers because of the mercies of God.
Our daily praise of God helps develop our friendship with Him.

Second, we should daily try to discover His secrets. Of
course, this means daily Bible study of some sort, because all of
God's secrets are contained in the Scripture. Friendship is based
on understanding. How shall we understand God if we are
ignorant of His character, His plans for this world, and His
promises?

Finally, we should expect God to be a friend to us. When
Abraham was asked to sacrifice Isaac, he was certainly faced
with a dilemma. We do not know much about his frame of mind
during his journey to Moriah, but the Book of Hebrews tells us
that he was "reasoning" about it. He had it all worked out that
if he went through with his act of obedience, "God could raise
the dead" (11:19). His knowledge of God's power and of His
friendship allowed him to go to the very point of sacrifice, so
that "figuratively speaking, he did receive Isaac back from
death" (v. 19).

Isaac is often ignored in this story. But here was a teenager (at
least) who allowed all these things to be done to him without a

recorded word of protest! Had not Abraham been a faithful father to "direct his children and his household after him to keep the way of the Lord" (Gen. 18:19)? Isaac, too, was a friend of God!

Selected Hymns

Listed below are hymns that stress the friendship of God. The references enclosed in parentheses indicate stanzas declaring God's friendship as found in the *Trinity Hymnal*. Other hymnals may have different versifications.

> "O Worship the King" (5)
> "O Could I Speak the Matchless Worth" (4)
> "O Sacred Head, Now Wounded" (3)
> "I Love Thy Kingdom, Lord" (5)
> "Jesus, and Shall It Ever Be" (4)
> "Jesus! What a Friend for Sinners" (1 and refrain)
> "I've Found a Friend, O Such a Friend" (all)
> "What a Friend We Have in Jesus" (1)
> "How Sweet the Name of Jesus Sounds" (4)
> "Jesus, Priceless Treasure" (1)
> "O Jesus, I Have Promised" (3)
> "Be Still, My Soul" (1)
> "Jesus Is All the World to Me" (all)
> "Jesus May Come Today" (1)
> "'Tis So Sweet to Trust in Jesus" (4)

6. Husband

"Till death us do part" is a portion of the marriage ceremony not taken seriously in many quarters today, even though it forms part of a vow made "before God and these witnesses." Yet that promise mirrors God's attitude toward His wayward people down through the ages. Since He promised to be the God of Abraham and his seed forever, again and again He returns to that promise to express His love for the true children of the patriarch.

Up to this point in our study we have been looking at God's love from different points of view. It is a love characterized by understanding (father), by delight and compassion (mother), by mutual experience (brother), and by mutual interest and of self-effacement (friend). In this chapter we look at God's love under the figure of earthly marriage. William Hendriksen has written that the union of Christ and His church is "such [an] intimate fellowship that no earthly metaphor can ever do justice to it. But . . . this marvelous love . . . is actually reflected here on earth in the union of a husband and his wife."[1]

Because human marriage has been chosen to reveal God's love for His people, it must be guarded against every attempt to distort it. Since God wishes to preserve its sacred character, Satan is using every wile and stratagem to distort and even

43

destroy it. Hence in this chapter we have two aims: to present God's love under the figure of a marriage being tested by satanic attacks and to underscore God's determination not to allow those attacks to dissolve permanently the bonds of His marriage.

The union of Christ and His church was foreshadowed in the Old Testament under the figure of God and His wife, Israel. The prophets spoke of this relationship against the background of Israel's apostasy and of the Lord's determination to restore His people despite their rebellion and sin.

Isaiah 50:1

As the Lord spoke through Isaiah to explain the coming exile, He stooped to the level of His hearers to make the point that He was not to blame for their separation. In Deuteronomy 24, God had decreed certain rights of protection for a divorced woman, with the further proviso that she might not return to her first husband if she had married another after the divorce. Under these conditions a certificate of divorce proved that her first husband was really through with her and could never legally take her back.

Against this background God asked regarding Judah whether the nation was ever let go by Him. The answer was a resounding no. Judah could not produce a certificate of divorce issued by God because He no longer loved her. The apostasy was really her choice, but that did not dissolve the marriage. A reconciliation was still possible, and God, in the still distant future, would pursue His wayward wife.

Hosea 3:1

While Isaiah was speaking of Judah's apostasy, Hosea was dealing with a similar situation in the northern kingdom.

Many things are obscure in Hosea's prophecy, but 3:1 is clear enough. Hosea has had an unhappy marriage because Gomer, his wife, has gone after other husbands. Let us look at the indictment he brings against Gomer and, by implication, the nation Israel. We should make one observation regarding any interpretation of this part of Hosea. The relationship between Hosea and Gomer, and between God and Israel, is so intertwined that it is difficult to distinguish them. The writer seems to move from one to the other often without making mention of the fact.

The very language Hosea used shows the wickedness of the conduct of the wayward wife: "adulterous look . . . unfaithful. . . . children of adultery . . . conceived them in disgrace. . . . lewdness." In addition, "she has not acknowledged that I was the one who gave her the grain, the new wine and oil, who lavished on her the silver and gold—which they used for Baal"; "she burned incense to the Baals; she decked herself with rings and jewelry, and went after her lovers, but me she forgot" (2:1-13).

Even on the strictest interpretation of the law, Hosea (and God) would have clear grounds for immediate divorce, as well as immediate judgment upon the erring partner. But God had other plans for Gomer (and Israel), and so He spoke to Hosea. "Go, show your love to your wife again, though she is loved by another and is an adulteress. Love her as the Lord loves the Israelites, though they turn to other gods and love the sacred raisin-cakes" (3:1).

The Lord's pursuit of Israel would first entail bringing her to her senses:

> She said, "I will go after my lovers, . . ."
> Therefore I will block her path with thornbushes;
>   I will wall her in so that she cannot find her way. . . .
> Then she will say,
>   "I will go back to my husband as at the first."
> (2:5-7)

God blocked Israel's path by sending drought and depression, and then by sending the nation into exile. The details of these judgments are given in verses 9 to 13. But those events were also acts of grace. After the exile God's people would return to the land in the spirit with which some had left

Egypt and entered Canaan under Joshua (vv. 14-15):

> "In that day," declares the Lord,
>   "you will call me 'my husband'; ...
> I will betroth you to me forever;
>   I will betroth you in righteousness and justice,
>   in love and compassion.
> I will betroth you in faithfulness,
>   and you will acknowledge the Lord."
>
>   (vv. 16-20)

God's unswerving faithfulness to His oath and His covenant, though difficult to understand, is an example of His grace and of His determination to call out a people for His name.

Ezekiel 16:32

As the time drew nearer for Judah's exile, Ezekiel used the metaphor of marriage further to reveal God's grace and faithfulness to His covenant with the fathers.

Ezekiel 16 is one of the great Old Testament expositions of sovereign grace as the prophet, in an extended allegory, describes God's love and affection for the nation as His beloved from its very beginning. The nation's condition at its birth was pathetic: "your cord was not cut"; "no one looked on you with pity"; "you were thrown into an open field."

In the midst of this wretchedness, "I passed by ... and as you lay there in your blood I said to you, 'Live!'" (v. 6). "Later I passed by, and when I looked at you and saw that you were old enough for love,

> [1] I spread the corner of my garment over you
> [2] and covered your nakedness.
> [3] I gave you my solemn oath
> [4] and entered into a covenant with you,
> [5] ... and you became mine." (v. 8)

In their discussion of Ezekiel's allegory, Andersen and Freedman (*The Anchor Bible: Hosea*) calls these actions those of a bridegroom in his part of the wedding ceremony. This interpretation is strengthened by the fact that later on in the chapter God speaks of Israel as an adulterous wife, one who prefers strangers to her own husband (cf. vv. 32, 45). The "strangers" were the nations of Egypt, Assyria, and Babylonia (vv. 26, 28, 29).

The next paragraph in chapter 16 describes the gifts of love showered on the nation as the Lord in His providence cared for His bride in the wilderness and then gave her the rich and pleasant land for her habitation. Note the contrast between His love and her wretched faithlessness:

The Gifts He Gave Her (vv. 9-14)	*What She Did with Them* (vv. 15-19)
• embroidered dress, fine linen, costly garments (v. 10)	• decorated high places with them (v. 16)
• fine linen, costly fabric, embroidered cloth (v. 13)	• put them on idols (v. 18)
• jewelry: bracelets, necklace, ring, earrings, crown (vv. 11-12)	• made them into idols (v. 17)
• flour, honey, oil (v. 13)	• offered oil and food as sacrifices (v. 19)
• all these made her beautiful (vv. 13-14)	• used beauty and fame to become prostitute (v. 15)
• fame spread because of her beauty (vv. 13-14)	

Clearly, the import of these statements is to show God as a rejected lover, dismayed and even shocked at the perfidy of His wife.

The husband is angry and promises judgment on the faithless wife. "I will sentence you to the punishment of women who commit adultery" (v. 38; cf. Lev. 20:2; Num. 15:36; Deut. 22:21). God will choose Israel's lovers as the very ones who will carry out the judgment—a clear prediction of the exile and the events leading up to it. (We recall that the message of Jerusalem's fall did not reach Ezekiel until the events of chapter 33.)

Though severe, God's anger will not be permanent. "Then

my wrath against you will subside and my jealous anger will turn away from you; I will be calm and no longer angry" (v. 42). The husband will not give his wife up but will persevere in pursuing her.

Jeremiah 3:18

Jeremiah 3 parallels the message of Ezekiel 16. The prophet recalled the law of divorce in Deuteronomy 24 (v. 1), depicted Judah's apostasy as prostitution (vv. 2ff.), and spoke of God's future plans for the nation:

> "Return, faithless Israel," declares the Lord,
> "I will frown on you no longer,
> for I am merciful," declares the Lord,
> "I will not be angry forever."
>
> (Jer. 3:12)

God, the faithful husband, will restore His people, bring them to Zion, and give them shepherds after His own heart. The ark of the covenant will be forgotten because God Himself will sit enthroned in Zion, and the two nations, hitherto divided since the days of Rehoboam, will again be one. In this way, the alienation between the nations, and between God and His people, will be finally overcome. The divine husband has kept His vow despite the unfaithfulness of the wife. He has not only maintained the marriage, but has also renewed in the wife the faithfulness she has so sorely lacked. Where sin has abounded, grace will much more abound.

Notes
[1] Hendriksen, *Galatians and Ephesians*, 257.

Part Two

Inanimate Objects
as
Mirrors of His Glory

7. Rock

Israel is a rocky place. On a visit there, I heard the humorous remark that when God had finished His work of creation, He had a lot of rocks left over—and He proceeded to dump them all on the land of Israel.

There are all sorts of rocks: pebbles, boulders, rocky strata just under a thin layer of soil, mountains, hills, cliffs, and, of course, stone used for building. Most of these kinds have found their way into the biblical account as literal objects, while several kinds have been used figuratively to express the character and activities of the God of Israel.

We will focus our attention on the ways God compares Himself to a rock in the writings of Moses, David and some of the other psalmists, Isaiah, and Jesus and His apostles.

Deuteronomy 32:31

The people who gathered in the desert of Moab to listen to Moses' several farewell speeches were well acquainted with rocks of different kinds. So, when Moses referred to these rocks several times in his speech recorded in Deuteronomy 32, the Israelites could very well understand what he was talking about. On its way out of Egypt, God had given the previous generation water from a rock (Exod. 17:6), supplying the people's need even though they had grumbled in unbelief. This "rock" may have been a layer of rock, a large boulder, or the side of a mountain. In any case, the miracle left its imprint on the memories of the people (compare a similar miracle in Num. 20:2ff.).

The mountain of Sinai towered above the plain, often enveloped in clouds. In itself, it must have been an awesome sight. But when God gave evidences of His presence—the thick cloud, the trumpet blast, the smoke and fire, and perhaps an earthquake—the huge mountain became unforgettable. Later on, Moses was placed in a crevice of a rock on that very mountain as the glory of the Lord passed by.

Surely rocks were beginning to have a significant place in the events the people were experiencing with their God. The Israelites were learning the grace, the power, and the greatness of this God who had chosen them for Himself.

Now, as the children of the Exodus stood in the plains of Moab, they were amid mountains and rocky formations. So, Moses used the figure of a rock to remind the people of God's greatness, especially as seen in His faithfulness, and to contrast that attribute with their own waywardness and the ineffectiveness of the idols they had worshiped along the wilderness way.

Moses first of all proclaimed the "name of the Lord," a common Hebrew designation for the character of the Lord Himself. He is "the Rock, his works are perfect, and all his ways are just. A faithful God who does no wrong, upright and just is he" (vv. 3-4). The word *rock* properly describes the Lord, for like a rock, or mountain, He is immovable, not subject to changes and whims.

There is an instructive association of ideas here that should not be missed. A rock is stable and unmoving; therefore, it reminds us of the faithful God. Because He is faithful, He is upright and without flaw; therefore, He is reliable. Later on in the chapter God appeared as the "only" God, because other gods, the idols of other nations, have proved to be unreliable and unable to deliver the people who called on them (cf. vv. 30, 37-39).

God's faithfulness to His people is seen in their history (vv. 7-12). He brought them out of Egypt and met every one of their needs. He was also faithful to His covenant with them when they deserted Him and followed other gods—faithful, that is, in judging them and purging them of evildoers (vv. 15-26). God was faithful to His name and reputation, and He preserved them "lest the adversary misunderstand and say, 'Our hand has triumphed; the Lord has not done all this'" (v. 27).

Other instances of His faithfulness might be multiplied. A striking example of it accompanies Balak's attempt to have Balaam cast a curse on the unknowing and unsuspecting Israelites, who were passing by Moab at the time. Although he was bribed and often cajoled by Moab's king, Balaam proceeded to bless the people he was called upon to curse. His explanation: "Even if Balak gave me his palace filled with silver and gold, I could not do anything of my own accord, good or bad, to go beyond the command of the Lord—and I must say only what the Lord says" (Num. 24:13). Since the New Testament ascribes the depths of perfidy to Balaam (cf. 2 Pet. 2:15f.; Jude 11), we should not think of his actions as resulting from his piety but rather from the power of the sovereign God, who was faithful to His people even when they were unaware of danger.

Psalm 18:2

David was also acquainted with rocks and hills. He used them for hiding places when running away from Saul, who wanted to kill him. Some time after he was free from Saul and from the enemies surrounding Israel, David penned Psalm 18 (repeated as 2 Samuel 22), heaping up word after word to describe how God had delivered him:

> The Lord is my rock, my fortress and my deliverer;
>   my God is my rock, in whom I take refuge,
> He is my shield and the horn of my salvation, my stronghold.[1]
>   (v. 2f.)

A large rock is a good thing to hide behind. A high rock gives a natural advantage to a warrior seeking to defend himself. The cleft of a rock provides shelter from the elements as well as making detection difficult. So, when David put his trust in God, he discovered that he was safe from his enemies. "Day after day Saul searched for him, but God did not give David into his hands" (1 Sam. 23:14).

An interesting aspect of David's use of the word is that he thinks of God his rock as active, beyond the literal meaning of the word. David writes: "And who is the Rock except our God? It is God who arms me with strength. . . . He makes my feet like the feet of a deer. . . . He trains my hands for battle" (Ps. 18:31-34). Unlike a physical and passive rock, God actively took David's part in rescuing him and encouraging him. When David's men discovered that Amalekites had destroyed their camp at Ziklag and carried off their families, they were distraught: "They wept aloud until they had no strength to weep" (1 Sam. 30:4). Yet, they had enough strength to rebel against David's leadership to the point where they were ready to stone him! In this extremity David turned to the Lord as refuge, and he found "strength in the Lord his God" (v. 6).

Thus encouraged, and further strengthened by a revelation through the ephod, David and his men searched for the Amalekites. In the good providence of God, they found a young Egyptian, a slave of an Amalekite, who directed them to the marauders' camp. "Nothing was missing: young or old, boy or girl, plunder or anything else they had taken. David brought everything back" (v. 19). By means of this victory, David escaped being impoverished; but, perhaps more importantly for the future, he left an impressive reminder for the Philistines of his prowess as a general and warrior. Moreover, he was able to cement good relationships with his friends in Judah by sharing the booty with them (cf. vv. 26ff.).

David had one further "enemy" to contend with—a weakness in his own personality. It is a common saying that the Bible does not hide the imperfections of even its greatest saints. First Samuel 25 tells a story in which David's strength and weakness are apparent. A moving army, especially a fleeing one, requires constant replenishment for its food supply. In David's day, his men depended on local farmers for their kindness and generosity. David felt that Nabal would certainly help him, since his shearers had not been molested by David's men and had probably been protected by them during sheep-shearing time. Moreover, as a descendant of Caleb and thus a member of the covenant nation, Nabal was obliged by the law to permit passers-by to satisfy their hunger. Of course, to satisfy the hunger of several hundred warriors might take a lot of grain, but David left it to Nabal's judgment. Instead of helping, Nabal felt no obligation at all and replied with harsh words. "Who is this David? who is this son of Jesse? Many servants are breaking away from their masters these days. Why should I take my bread and water, and the meat I have slaughtered for my shearers, and give it to men coming from who knows where?" (vv. 10f.).

One harsh and rash word produced another. Infuriated, David ordered his men to take up weapons. "It's been useless—all my watching over this fellow's property in the desert so that nothing of his was missing. He has paid me back evil for good. May God deal with David, be it ever so severely, if by morning I leave alive one male of all who belong to him" (vv. 21f.).[2]

Several points should be noted here. First, David took an oath, thus bringing down upon himself judgment if he did not carry it out. Next, as to the content of the oath, he vowed to kill every male in Nabal's household. However much Nabal's reply was to be condemned, David's response went far beyond what the situation called for. It was the response of a hot-head, not that of a man after God's own heart and a future king of Israel.

In this situation God once again became a refuge and a deliverer. In His providence, Abigail, Nabal's wife, learned of the exchange between David and her husband. So she set out under cover with donkeys loaded with food. Meeting David and his men intent on their carnage, she dissuaded him from his hot-headed course of action with one of the most powerful statements for sobriety and self-control in all of the Bible (vv. 24-31). She recognized David's place in redemptive history and urged in view of that, "Let no wrongdoing be found in you as long as you live." Understanding something of God's protective power she predicted, "Even though someone is pursuing you to take your life, the life of my master will be bound securely in the bundle of the living by the Lord your God. But the lives of your enemies he will hurl away as from the pocket of a sling." Abigail concluded her admonition, "When the Lord has done for my master every good thing he has promised concerning him and has appointed him leader over Israel, my master will not have on his conscience the staggering burden of needless bloodshed or of having avenged himself" (v. 31).

Thus rebuked, David saw the wisdom in her counsel and broke off the intended raid on Nabal's estate. He saw God's hand in sending Abigail and delivering him from an act that would certainly have disqualified him from the kingship.

God, the unchangeable rock, had protected David and by His providence had seen to it that His purpose concerning David would find fulfillment.

Isaiah 28:16

On my daily walks to and from high school, I frequently passed a row of attractive, newly built houses in a growing part of the city. Except for the corner house, however, the row was never occupied. As time passed we could understand why. Slowly but surely the houses began to settle, their walls crack, and their windows shatter. Clearly, something was wrong with their foundations. The builder must have been greatly embarrassed, both in his reputation and in his finances. He had not built on rock.

Rocks may be immovable and sturdy; they may afford refuge in their clefts. When quarried and cut, they are useful in the construction of buildings, for they provide a solid foundation against the elements and the ravages of time (see Jesus' words in Matt. 7:24ff.).

Isaiah prophesied during a time when first Israel, then Judah, preferred foreign alliances to obedience to God's covenant. Weakened and quite helpless in the face of surrounding enemies, both nations made treaties with empires who promised help—but at a tremendous price. In chapter 28, the prophet first spoke of Israel's doom because the nation was trusting in Assyria (vv. 1-4), then predicted that Judah would suffer a similar fate because the nation was trusting in Egypt. The problem with Judah was now more than disobedience; a certain cynicism had set in among the leaders, who made fun of Isaiah by mocking his messages:

> Who is it he is trying to teach?
>> To whom is he explaining his message?
> To children weaned from their milk,
>> to those just taken from the breast?
> For it is:
>> Do and do, do and do,
>> rule on rule, rule on rule;
>> a little here, a little there.
>
> (vv. 9f.)

Because they had refused Isaiah's clear words in the Hebrew language, the leaders of Judah would hear the Babylonian language spoken in their midst when soldiers would invade the land to destroy it (v. 11). Clearly the children of Judah mocked Isaiah because they had confidence in Egypt. They expressed their boast in playful language (or perhaps in their departure from God they had really covenanted with death and hell for protection):

> You boast, "We have entered into a covenant with death,
>> with the grave we have made an agreement.
> When an overwhelming scourge sweeps by,
>> it cannot touch us,
> for we have made a lie our refuge
>> and falsehood our hiding place."
>
> (v. 15)

Now, in contrast to the false confidence afforded by foreign alliances or even covenants with death, God was providing a structure that would endure, whose adherents would never be ashamed (v. 16). This building stone is tested, held in honor, and

capable of sustaining all the weight placed on it. Isaiah's
hearers may well have been reminded of the Davidic covenant with its promise of an everlasting dynasty, provided
only that the kings obey the covenant stipulations and lead
the people to do so.

However, in Isaiah's day this very obedience was lacking,
and later on the dynasty was discontinued because king after
king refused to hear the prophets' warnings. The New Testament
writers, as we shall soon see, understood that Jesus the Messiah
is the true stone. He is the true son of David, not only the
fulfillment of the promise but also the faithful keeper of its
provisions (Rom. 9:33; 10:11; 1 Cor. 3:11; Eph. 2:20; 1 Pet. 2:4, 6).

Isaiah 8:14

Up to this point in our chapter, rocks and stones have been
symbols of encouragement, reminding us that God is faithful,
He is our refuge, and He is thoroughly reliable. Because Isaiah
had a mixed audience of both believers and hypocrites, it
became necessary for him to speak of negative things, of
stumbling, of being broken and captured.

Chapter 8 is part of a section written during the reign of Ahaz,
one of the most disobedient and hypocritical of Judah's kings.
On the one hand he was endeavoring to placate an angry Isaiah
with a show of piety (7:12); on the other he was binding himself
and the nation to fealty to Assyria in exchange for protection
from Israel and Syria. It is no wonder that Jerusalem was
buzzing with gossip and speculation. God spoke to these people
through Isaiah, urging those who would listen to change their
ways and not follow the crowd:

> Do not call conspiracy
>   everything that these people call conspiracy;
> do not fear what they fear,
>   and do not dread it.
> The Lord Almighty is the one you are to regard as holy,
>   he is the one you are to fear,
>   he is the one you are to dread,[3]

and he will be a sanctuary;
  but for both houses of Israel he will be
a stone that causes men to stumble
  and a rock that makes them fall.

(Isa. 8:12-14)

How can God be both a sanctuary and a stumbling stone at the same time? Oswalt puts it beautifully: "The attitude we take toward God will determine what aspect of him we will experience. To those who sanctify him, who give him a place of importance in their lives, who seek to allow his character to be duplicated in them, he becomes a sanctuary, a place of refuge and peace. But to those who will not give him such a place in their lives, he becomes a stone to trip over."[4]

The point is that all of us are somewhat uncomfortable with God. We like to keep Him out of our lives or, at best, at arm's length. This is what Ahaz in particular and Judah in general were trying to do, because the demands of the covenant obedience had become inconvenient and even irritating. Isaiah's message is simply that God will not go away. No matter what circumstances arise, we still have to deal with Him both in the near present and in the distant future.

The consequences of trying to avoid God's claims are frightening, as expressed in the language of verses 14 and 15: "stumble," "fall," "trap," "snare," "broken," "snared," "captured." Isaiah gives real substance to these terms in verses 21 and 22:

> Distressed and hungry, they will roam through the land; when they are famished, they will become enraged and, looking upward, will curse their king and their God. Then they will look toward the earth and see only distress and darkness and fearful gloom, and they will be thrust into utter darkness.

This, and more, is the predicted stumbling over the Rock that will not go away.

Psalm 118

Most of the references in the Psalms repeat the nuances of faithfulness and refuge we have already studied. However

Psalm 118 adds a new thought to the cluster of ideas surrounding the images of "rock" and "stone." This psalm seems to have been written at the time of celebration at Jerusalem, expressing the faith and hope of pilgrims singing as they traveled. The psalmist, along with others, has gained a significant victory. He was snatched from the clutches of death, and he now wishes to go to Jerusalem to proclaim what the Lord has done.

Arriving at the city gate or perhaps the temple gate (v. 19), the psalmist seemed to engage in conversation with some of the city dwellers. He told of his victory over his enemies and used the following metaphor to describe it:

> The stone the builders rejected
>   has become the capstone;
> the Lord has done this,
>   and it is marvelous in our eyes.
> This is the day the Lord has acted;[5]
>   let us rejoice and be glad in it.

> (vv. 22-24)

In the context of the psalm, "stone" seems to refer to the writer himself. He may have been a king, an honored leader, or a poet celebrating the nation's victory. He had suffered temporary defeat and rejection, but he was now vindicated and triumphant. The comparison may have been suggested by a stone lying near the psalmist's path, left over after the building was completed and now lying unused and useless. The psalmist felt that his single triumph was symbolic of the ultimate victory Israel would enjoy over the nations.

However behind this struggle and victory lies the conflict between God and Satan. In that conflict Satan is granted much freedom and seemingly wins many victories. There are periods of time when the world as a whole will have nothing to do with God its Creator. Individuals, too, reject the sovereign and gracious rule of the Lord and disdain His grace. But the ultimate triumph is the Lord's. Along the way to that great day, His Gospel wins many a reversal. The lives of Paul, Augustine, and Newton are examples of this. The revivals of the eighteenth century in Britain and the United States are also part of this pattern. This is one reason why the discerning Christian never gives up hope. The stone may have been rejected, but it will be the cornerstone.

The New Testament

Jesus, Paul, and Peter have shown the real connection between Psalm 118 and Isaiah 8 and 28. See how these passages have been quoted as if they were but one (Matt. 21:42-44; Rom. 9:33; 1 Pet. 2:4-8). Much of the Old Testament is typical of New Testament reality. Thus, *Jesus* is *the* true Israel, *the* obedient servant, *the* seed of Abraham, and David's greater son. He is also the God-appointed foundation stone (1 Cor. 3:11; Eph. 2:20)—rejected or ignored by the people of His time, rejected or ignored by countless numbers ever since. But by the resurrection from the dead, He has become the cornerstone of God's kingdom in the world. Under the entry for "cornerstone," the *Oxford English Dictionary* quotes Isaac Watts: "the largest and fairest building sinks . . . to the ground, if the foundations and cornerstones of it are feeble and insufficient." Such is the importance of a cornerstone. The hope of every Christian rests on Jesus, and that hope is secure because He was raised from the dead.

Because we live in a wicked world, Jesus the cornerstone is also a stumbling stone who will not go away when the world wants Him to. This is the message of Isaiah 8:14, as we have seen, and 1 Peter 2:8. In reading these passages, Kapelrud suggests that we are to think of one who is traveling at night and might stumble over stones and fall.[6] To reject the Gospel is to choose to walk in darkness, and in that darkness one can only fall.

Peter has the final word for all who believe:

> See, I lay a stone in Zion,
>   a chosen and precious cornerstone,
> and the one who trusts in him
>   will never be put to shame.
>
> (1 Pet. 2:6)

This great stone has all the characteristics of the Old Testament "rock"—faithful, stabile, a hiding place, and confidence inspiring.

Notes

[1] It should be noted that the word *rock* translates two different Hebrew words similar in meaning.

[2] The NIV here follows some Septuagint MSS. The Hebrew reads, "May God deal with David's enemies, be it ever so severely...." For a comment on the passage following the Hebrew text, see Keil and Delitzsch.

[3] The personal pronouns used throughout vv. 12-13 are all second person plural (*you*).

[4] *The Book of Isaiah, Chapters 1-39* (NICOT), 234.

[5] I am departing from the translation of the NIV and other English versions. In my judgment the rendering given is much more in keeping with the sense of the context.

[6] TDOT, 1:51.

8. Refuge

Picture young David on the run. He had comforted Saul with his sweet music on the harp, served him successfully in his army, and married his daughter Michal. It should have been well with the young shepherd boy, but all these advantages were over-shadowed by the all-consuming jealousy of the king. Saul twice threw his spear at David, frequently sent him into battle hoping for his death, and once sent soldiers to take his life while he was in bed. Clearly David had to run for many months, seeking refuge from the would-be murderer and his army.

David sought shelter among the Philistines, in Moab, in the hill country of Judah, in caves, fortified cities, and mountain strongholds. When he left one haven in the morning, his first thought was, How will I be able to keep out of Saul's clutches? The odds were clearly against him. Not only did he have a small rag-tag group of misfits to fight against the seasoned army of the king, but everywhere he went people would be happy to turn him over to Saul and his pleasure. David was running for his life.

From these experiences David learned the importance of refuges. After he became king he and his successors saw to it that every large town was fortified so that the people would be protected. The fact is that God's people always have enemies and need to protect themselves. Except for the brief period of the reigns of David and Solomon when there was comparative peace and prosperity (1 Kings 4:20-21, 24-25), the cities in the Promised Land could expect raids, sieges, and other warlike acts from surrounding nations, both large and small. An Israelite city without fortifications simply would not survive.

When word came to Nehemiah in exile in Susa that the walls of Jerusalem had been broken down and its gates burned with fire, he understood that the plight of the city was great indeed. He wrote, "I sat down and wept. For some days I mourned and fasted and prayed before the God of heaven" (1:4).

The Hebrews had a variety of words to describe the fortifications of their time. Writers of the Bible used many of them to describe God as their refuge.

1 Samuel 22

The term "stronghold" appears in the narratives of David's wandering when Saul was pursuing him. The name Masada is probably derived from the Hebrew word translated "stronghold." It apparently indicates a mountain height, or a rocky crag, on which a defense of some sort had been erected. As David sought and found refuge in such places, he was safe from Saul's murderous intentions.

First Samuel 22 teaches an important lesson. When David was forced to flee from Saul and his men, the welfare of his parents became a great personal concern, lest Saul vent his frustration on them. So, David went to the king of Moab, because David himself was a descendant of Ruth, the Moabitess. He asked the king to protect his parents until he could receive a clearer revelation of God's purposes for all of them. David and his men found refuge in a stronghold in Moab, but this was not to be permanent. A prophet, Gad, told David to leave and go across the Jordan into the land of Judah. The reason seemed to be that David, as the anointed king, was to find his lasting safety in the land God had given His people. In other words, God and His providential control would be David's true stronghold and that control would be exercised in the land of Israel.

Psalm 62

David's enemies used various weapons in their attempts to destroy him and his kingdom. In this psalm, David was faced by a band of gossips. We do not know the particular circumstances, but there are many times in David's life when events and experiences described in a psalm may have taken place. David felt helpless before these gossip-mongers and their charges. He felt like a "leaning wall" and "a tottering fence" (v. 3). Their intent was plain: to "topple him from his lofty place" by lies and cursings.

David's recourse was to God alone. "My hope comes from him. He alone is my rock and my salvation; he is my fortress, I will not be shaken" (vv. 5-6). With God as his refuge, David could see how truly frail his enemies were. "If weighed in the balance, they are nothing; together they are only a breath" (v. 9). David's confidence was in God's righteous judgment:

> One thing God has spoken,
>   two things have I heard:
> that you, O God, are strong,
>   and that you, O Lord, are loving.
> Surely you will reward each person
>   according to what he has done.

(vv. 11-12)

David surely had his detractors, and just as surely they came to a just end. Absalom, Ahithophel, Shimei, and Adonijah were judged, while David was cleared. Because God was his fortress, David was not shaken.

There are times when liars must be refuted. A case in point is the slanders directed against Paul during his ministry. He refers to them in the Book of Galatians and in the Corinthian letters. And he goes to great lengths to answer them, because the lies were affecting the faith of the new believers. In such a case, untruths must be cleared up. But when Christians spend all their time trying to set every record straight, what time is left for the preaching of the Gospel and the nurture of the saints? Paul's counsel in Romans 12 should be noted. "Do not take revenge, my friends, but leave room for God's wrath, for it is written: 'It is mine to avenge; I will repay,' says the Lord" (v. 19).

Psalm 46

In the Bible, "fortress" sometimes refers to a city with high walls, fortified gates, and towers. Often within the city itself there would be a tower, a citadel, or castle. Such defenses were not always successful, especially against armies of the larger nations, but they were the best defense available, and people had to put their trust in them.

In Hezekiah's day, Sennacherib, king of Assyria, attacked and captured all the fortified cities of Judah. Whatever fortifications the Jews had, they were not sufficient protection against the Assyrian armies. Then Sennacherib turned his attention toward Jerusalem, and sent one of his commanders to try to talk the inhabitants into surrender, thus avoiding the necessity for a frontal assault or a long siege. As one reads Isaiah 36 and 37 (or 2 Kings 18-20), one understands that the defenses of Jerusalem were no match for the Assyrian king. Only God could deliver His city. And this is exactly what Isaiah promised Hezekiah:

> "He will not enter this city
>   or shoot an arrow here.
> He will not come before it with shield
>   or build a siege ramp against it.
> By the way that he came he will return;
>   he will not enter this city," declares the Lord.
> "I will defend this city and save it,
>   for my sake and for the sake of David my servant."
>   (Isa. 37:33ff.)

In response to this deliverance (or to ones similar to it), Psalms 46 and 48 were composed. The refrain of the former—"the God of Jacob is our fortress" (vv. 7, 11)—indicates the psalmist's conviction that where human defenses could (and often did) fail, God never failed the people living in the city of God.

The Lord is described as a refuge and source of strength; as such He is an ever present help when trouble appears. When in ancient times a besieging army appeared, the citizens of the city brought their families and all their property within the city walls, and then the gates were closed. A waiting game set in, as the city watched to see what the attackers would do. During this time of waiting, endurance and patience were needed, lest the people grow weary and lose heart. So they had to have confidence in their defenses, especially the walls and water supply. They could live serenely for a time even though the outside world might be in great upheaval. All these qualities the psalmist transferred to God the fortress and to the people who trusted in Him (vv. 1-3).

The Old Testament speaks of the importance of water for any fortified city (see 2 Kings 20:20; Isa. 7:3 where Ahaz, out of fear of an attack from the Syro-Israelitish alliance, was inspecting the water supply). With adequate quantities of water, a city might hold out indefinitely. In the city of God, there is a river flowing from the throne of God. It supplies water in such abundance that the citizens are happy and at peace (see more on water in chap. 10). They "will not fear."

God is not an outsider to the city. He dwells in His city. He has chosen to place His Name in the temple, and He lives as a citizen among the city dwellers (v. 4). Of course, He has done this since Sinai when His glory appeared and rested between the cherubim in the tabernacle. He was with His people during their travels in the desert—supplying them with what they needed, fighting their battles for them—and by His presence making them different from all the other nations of the earth.

His presence is not passive, but active (v. 5b). And although His presence is felt within the city, He is also active outside, among the nations to rule and subdue them. Verses 5 and 6 may well be a reference to the havoc God worked among the Assyrians in response to Hezekiah's prayer (cf. Isa. 36-37). "When the people got up the next morning—there were all the dead bodies!" (37:36). Sennacherib returned to Nineveh, where his sons assassinated him. Truly,

> Nations are in uproar, kingdoms fall;
> he lifts his voice, the earth melts.
>
> (Ps. 46:6)

God has invited the nations of the world, whether they pay attention or not, to examine what He has done. He is a God of war, and He is the God who brings peace (vv. 8-9). The nations are not only invited to contemplate God's mighty acts in the world, they are also invited to know that He is God who will be exalted among them. What He did to Sennacherib and his army is only a symbol of the worldwide destruction He will bring on the earth (v. 10).

But Israel must also hear and consider. A danger lurked in the nation's path: to think that God would stay among them even though they were persisting in hypocrisy and wickedness. God's covenant with Jacob has two sides. There is the side of His promise of protection and grace, and the side of the people's obedience and fidelity to the covenant. As Jeremiah was to make clear, the people could not use the temple as a rabbit's foot or a horseshoe (chap. 7). They would have to show a holiness of heart and life as the effect of God's dwelling among them. And Ezekiel was to see the Spirit leaving the temple in Jerusalem because of the wickedness within (chap. 11). The message "Be still, and know that I am God" was for Jerusalem's ears as well as for the nations.

Psalm 61

Towers served a variety of purposes in ancient Israel. There were watchtowers for the oversight of flocks and herds (Mic. 4:8) or of vineyards (Isa. 5:2); watchtowers on city walls to detect the approach of strangers, either friendly or hostile (2 Kings 9:17); towers for offensive war (perhaps the structure at Siloam served this purpose [Luke 13:4]), and towers for defense (note the structures mentioned in Neh. 3). As to towers for defensive purposes, there were towers on city walls as a primary line of defense and towers within the walls as a final refuge against the enemy.

Sometime after he became king, David called on God for help. He was at "the ends of the earth." This expression might be construed literally, for David did have to cross Jordan when he fled from Absalom; or it might be interpreted figuratively, for he felt desperately in need. Faint at heart, David asked God to give him the encouragement and stability a rock would afford (vv. 1-2).

David had real confidence in God, "for you have been my refuge, a strong tower against the foe." In fact, more than most people in the Old Testament, he could attest to God's protecting providence, as we have already seen in this and preceding chapters. His foes make quite a list: a lion and a bear, the Philistines, Saul, the Amalekites, Absalom, Shimei, Ahithophel, and Mephibosheth. David's knowledge of God's acts of faithfulness in the past encouraged him to believe in His protection in the future.

But a more powerful foe seemed to be facing David in this psalm. Since his request went beyond an ordinary lifetime ("forever" vv. 4, 7; "many generations" v. 6), it seems proper to infer that David was also concerned with the ultimate enemy, death. Perhaps that was why, although his cry came from the ends of the earth, David desired to return to Jerusalem and in particular to the tent in which the ark of the covenant resided. There his true salvation lay, and there he found God as a strong tower against the foe.

We fear death because it is unnatural. We fear it because it is unknown and strange. We fear death because it is the wages for sin and for sinful living. Our fear leads to a feeling of helplessness and despair. But at the mercy seat above the ark we find forgiveness and the assurance that God is with us. To dwell there forever is to rest serene "in the shelter of your wings, O God" (v. 4). (On the figure of wings, see the comments under "Bird" in chap. 16). We may not be clear about many of the details of the afterlife, but we may have confidence that the God who has been our strong tower in this life will not forsake us in the life to come.

God is a strong tower for those who put their trust in Him. This biblical image leads us to a passage in Proverbs.

Proverbs 18:10

> The name of the Lord is a strong tower;
> the righteous run to it and are safe.

Like many names in the Old Testament, God's name is much more than a mere denominative. It is an expression of His character, and the phrase "name of the Lord" is often another way of designating the Lord Himself. We see this in the passage where God spoke of His name "Yahweh." In Exodus 3, the Lord commissioned Moses as the leader of the Israelites. Part of Moses' reluctance to accept that appointment was his fear that the people would not recognize God and would be unwilling to follow Moses:

> Suppose I go to the Israelites and say to them, "The God of your fathers has sent me to you," and they ask me, "What is his name?" then what shall I tell them? (v. 13)

To this question, the Lord responded:

> I am who I am. This is what you are to say to the Israelites: "I AM has sent me to you. . . ." This is my name forever, the name by which I am to be remembered from generation to generation. (vv. 14, 15)

Thousands of words have been written speculating on the meaning of the name. Doubtless there is some truth in most of these suggestions. However it is difficult to believe that a nation of uneducated slaves would be able to follow the abstract reasoning in most of them. And the Israelites were such uneducated slaves. What they needed to know from Moses was that God really was and that He could do what He had just promised. The new name expressed God's reality to them and His freedom to challenge Pharaoh's rule. The plagues that followed were a confirmation that I AM and that the Egyptian gods AIN'T!

So, when faithful Israelites invoked that sacred name, they discovered that Yahweh was God not only at the time of the Exodus but at any moment of their own lives when an enemy attacked. We have already seen an instance of this during the reign of Hezekiah (see comments under Psalm 46 above). An equally striking example is seen earlier during the time of

Jehoshaphat. The Moabites, Ammonites, and others were ready to attack Jerusalem. The king proclaimed a fast, and many came from other parts of the realm "to seek help from the Lord" (2 Chron. 20:1ff.). Rising to address all the people in the front of the new courtyard of the temple, Jehoshaphat said, "O Lord . . . " Of course, it is easy just to mouth God's name as a concession to religion or to speak it without much thought. But the earnestness with which Jehoshaphat prayed belies either interpretation. He was uttering the name of the Lord as he recalled God's mighty acts in the past, deeds that showed God is the living and true God.

The king reviewed the nation's history and God's faithfulness during the conquest. He reminded the Lord that the very temple he was standing in was built as a sanctuary for His name and that the people had vowed, "If calamity comes upon us, whether the sword of judgment, or plague or famine, we will stand in your presence before this temple that bears your Name and will cry out to you in our distress, and you will hear us and save us." So, Jehoshaphat continued to pray, averring helplessness, but calling upon the Lord in hope.

Of course God heard. The enemies fought among themselves until their military power was destroyed. The armies of Judah did not need to fight; they spent their energies picking up the loot! "On the fourth day (after the battle was first joined) they assembled in the Valley of Beracah [the name means "praise"], where they praised the Lord" (v. 26). The righteous, following the lead of their righteous king, had run into a strong tower and were safe.

Many biblical proverbs are set as isolated statements, having little or nothing to do with the verses that precede or follow. But it is tempting to connect our verse with the one following it:

> The wealth of the rich is their fortified city;
> they imagine it an unscalable wall.
>
> (18:11)

Here again we have an image borrowed from the military. Again we have the thought of trusting in a higher power for security. An unscalable wall is not unlike a high tower. Yet, one of the great themes of Wisdom Literature is that wealth does not offer much security:

> Wealth is worthless in the day of wrath,
>> but righteousness delivers from death.
>>>> (Prov. 11:4)

And there are many more. These two proverbs have been juxtaposed to show the superficial power of riches against the security the child of God finds in his High Tower.

9. Shield

As the saying goes, "You don't kick people when they're down." Of course, the world does and sometimes the saints do, too. And Satan certainly does. Take the case of David when he was under chastening for his adultery and murder. He could rejoice in God's forgiveness (2 Sam. 12:13), but he also had to bear the punishment announced by Nathan (vv. 10ff.).

Neither David's sins nor their punishments were secret things. The Israelites and perhaps their neighbors knew of both, and their tongues wagged. Was it not the sweet singer of Israel, the man after God's own heart, who had done these wicked things?

The crowning blows came upon David with the rebellion of Absalom, the treachery of Ahithophel, and the cursing of Shimei (2 Sam. 15-18). Forced to flee, David left Jerusalem, "weeping as he went; his head was covered and he was barefoot" (15:30). He arrive at his destination exhausted (16:14). Was this the great king of Israel? These punishments were harsh enough in themselves, but David's enemies taunted, "God will not deliver him" (Ps. 3:2). Clearly, David had Judah with him, but did he have the Lord?

So David went to the Lord in the prayer uttered in Psalm 3. He described his desperate situation (vv. 1f.). He was confident that God was his shield and the one "who lifts up my head" (v. 3). A person who has failed needs two things: *protection* during the time of discouragement and the weakness that accompanies it and *encouragement* to believe that he or she can begin again. In David's case both the protection and encouragement came in the form of human comradeship. In quick succession, Ittai, Zadok, Hushai, and Ziba (2 Sam. 15, 16), not to mention Joab and Abishai, rallied to David's side. Just as quickly the tide turned. Absalom was led by Hushai to follow a disastrous strategy in pursuing David, and the battle was soon over. David returned to Jerusalem, to his throne, and to rule in the hearts of all the people. But God had been his shield and had lifted up his head.

The lesson in all this is obvious. God often uses people to protect and encourage the downcast. When repentance is genuine and full, the backsliders in our churches need the comfort of a shield, so that they may recover from their transgression and the fallout that inevitably accompanies it and get on with their lives.

In the above example, we saw that shielding David was only a part of what God did for him. A shield by itself is never enough for a soldier. It will protect in a limited sort of way, but it has no value in meeting other needs in the battle. Consider the following Scriptures where God is called our shield in company with something else:

- shield and reward (Gen. 15:1)
- shield and help(er) (Deut. 33:29; Ps. 33:20; 115:9-11)
- strength and shield (Ps. 28:7)
- sun and shield (Ps. 84:11)
- shield and the word (Ps. 18:30; Prov. 30:5)
- shield and a list of other protections (Ps. 18:2; 144:2).

Limited in its usefulness, the shield is nonetheless important in warfare. In earlier chapters we have seen God as rock, refuge, horn, eagle, and warrior—all metaphors for protection of a general sort. We must see His work as shield in a specific way. He protects against enemies, and since our warfare is essentially spiritual, His protection is against "all flaming arrows of the evil one" (Eph. 6:16).

Let us consider what Scripture says about Satan and his angels. First, they are a well-organized body ("an organically coherent unity," to quote one author). They are likened to a kingdom and a household with Satan as the "prince" (Matt. 12:25f.), and God has given them an amazingly vast territory to control (1 John 5:18f.).

Second, Satan and his angels have some power in their struggle against the saints. In Daniel 10, demons had the power to resist an angel sent with the answer to Daniel's prayer (v. 13); the answer was delayed for three weeks because of this demonic opposition.

Peter had boasted that he would not forsake Jesus in a moment of trial. Jesus then told Peter that Satan had prayed to have the disciple "to sift you as wheat" (Luke 22:31)—and God had granted the request! Peter was sifted and found wanting, but Jesus' prayer brought his restoration (v. 32). Satan found ways to "stop" Paul from revisiting the Thessalonians (1 Thess. 2:18) and tried to make his life miserable with a thorn in the flesh (2 Cor. 12:7). These activities, an outworking of God's eternal purpose, can also be ascribed to Him. (Consider the parallel passages 2 Sam. 24:1 and 1 Chron. 21:1). Yet there can be no doubt that Satan's acts are real and terrifying.

In this struggle the saints are definitely at risk. Satan seems to be a creature of greater-than-human wisdom, and in addition he is an experienced warrior, having been at it for thousands of years. Left to ourselves we should easily be outwitted. These facts make the teaching of God our shield all the more meaningful and practical.

God shields us by giving us needed information. The old adage "Forewarned is fore-armed" offers good advice. That is why David and Agur (who seemed to quote David) spoke of the Word in connection with a shield (Ps. 18:30; Prov. 30:5):

> Every word of God is flawless;
>   he is a shield to those who take refuge in him.

Agur adds appropriately,

> Do not add to his words,
>   or he will rebuke you and prove you a liar.

This is probably the meaning of the words of Psalm 84:11:

> . . . the Lord God is a sun and shield.

When we walk in the daylight afforded by God's Word, we are able to see traps and stumbling blocks Satan has put in our way. Paul was aware of these when he urged the Corinthians to show forgiveness to the repentant member of their church. Satan could and would use their pride and arrogance to destroy what he had done in their midst. So forgiveness was indicated "in order that Satan might not outwit us. For we are not unaware of his schemes" (2 Cor. 2:11).

The Scriptures alert us to some of those schemes. In this day and age we are easily seduced by a nice personality and an apparently loving countenance. Satan and his servants "masquerade as servants of righteousness" (2 Cor. 11:13ff.), even though underneath they are "false apostles, deceitful workmen, masquerading as apostles of Christ." How often have the saints been shielded from such people by taking heed to the Scriptures and testing everything by them (1 Thess. 5:21).

In Abraham's case, "shield" is accompanied by "reward" (Gen. 15:1). Humanly speaking, he had reason to be afraid. The patriarch had just defeated four powerful chieftains, but would they regroup and attack again? Or would Abraham's success breed envy in his neighbors' hearts and would he suffer from them? After all, he was the alien among the Amorites, and acceptance never comes easy, especially when opposing religions and cultures are concerned. Abraham remained an outsider and was in constant need of protection from lurking animosities. So God said, "Do not be afraid, Abram."

Perhaps Abram also needed shielding from himself. His recent success in battle was matched by his success as a herdsman, and he was now the owner of vast possessions (cf. Gen. 13:5f.). The temptation to let his prosperity "go to his head" would have been a great one to this new convert to the Lord. He might lose sight of all that the covenant promised him—"the city with foundations, whose architect and builder is God" (Heb. 11:10)—and settle for the best Canaan could offer. So God reminded him that He was also Abraham's great reward (as Matthew Henry points out, "not only thy rewarder, but thy reward"). There is always something better than the gifts God gives, and that something is God Himself. Moses resisted the same temptation when he insisted on more than success in defeating the Canaanites; he would rather stay in the wilderness with God than gain the land without Him (Exod. 33:14ff.; cf. Ps. 73:25f.).

Thus "shield" and "reward" go hand in hand: the Shield is the Reward, and the Reward is the Shield.

As we noted previously, a shield is defensive armor and needs an active accompaniment. As Moses reviewed the history of Israel, he thought of God as helper as well as shield (Deut. 33:26-29). He had ridden on the heavens above to help His people, and underneath were His everlasting arms. He would give Israel victory over the nations of Canaan, so that the Israelites might dwell in safety alone, with well-watered fields and vineyards. Samuel celebrated a fulfillment of this promise when he named the stone Ebenezer, for "thus far has the Lord helped us" (1 Sam. 8:12).

The writer of Psalm 33 also unites the thoughts of shield and help. His is a song of praise for the truth and power of His Word (vv. 1-11) and for the perfection of His judgment in behalf of the nation whose God is the Lord (vv. 12-19). That nation is delivered not by the size of its army but by its trust in God and His unfailing love. It cannot protect itself alone. God must be its help and shield.

Psalm 115 may be an antiphonal song, written for public worship. It is one of the so-called Hallel Psalms used in liturgies connected with Passover and the Feast of Tabernacles. Such psalms may have been sung by our Lord and the disciples on

Passover evening (Matt. 26:30). It begins with words of praise to God for His love and faithfulness. It shows in detail how God differs from idols of the nations: they can do nothing, while He does what He pleases. This is an obvious reference to the Exodus and the contest with Egypt's gods.

After such a beginning, the psalm turns to encourage the Israelites to trust Him, for "he is their help and shield" (vv. 9-11). The appeal is to the unchangeableness of God. He had helped them during the Exodus, shielding them from Pharaoh, and He will help and shield them both now and in the future. Not only individual Israelites, but the priestly family and the Levites must also trust; they are not exempt from Satan's attacks but, in fact, are all the more vulnerable to them. And then there are the proselytes, the "God fearers." These have a unique set of problems because they are new to many scriptural practices and are often tempted to return to their old ways. They are exhorted to trust in God their help and shield.

We may feel a little strange in speaking of God as a helper. Plumbers often have helpers, young men learning the trade who do menial tasks like turning off the water or going for a wrench. The word *helper* need not be taken in that sense, although we should note that many times God does condescend to be with us and bear our burdens. But God presents Himself as helper to balance another proper view of His absolute sovereignty. When thinking of His sovereignty we are sometimes tempted to do nothing because we know He does it all. I once had a student who said he had not prayed for two years because God was sovereign and, thus, prayer was not needed. I am glad he is praying today.

There is a balance between sovereignty and human responsibility. God's covenants place certain demands on us, and we must carry them out. When we do so, He assures He will help us with wisdom and power and will protect us from the mistakes that lurk along the way.

The Helper gives strength, and this is the testimony of Psalm 28:6 and 8. The psalmist was in some kind of trouble and feared the wicked, the hypocrites, those who did not regard the works of the Lord. He prayed for deliverance from them (vv. 1-5). His prayer was answered, and he praised God for His mercy. God had been a shield and a source of strength (vv. 6f.).

God is always a shield for His people, but often our strength is dissipated and must be renewed. In particular, the struggle against wicked people and the powers of evil, often long and drawn-out, can be debilitating. Christians frequently suffer "burn out" and totally exhaust their strength. Sometimes renewal comes in the form of a "second wind." A distance runner knows he or she will feel complete exhaustion and every part of the body will cry out to stop running. But there is a secret to be learned: keep running for a few more yards because the feeling of exhaustion will pass and new strength will be experienced. Often Christians need just to keep going, and they will experience a spiritual "second wind." God will revive their spirits and bodies in the normal course of their activities. Perhaps this happened to David (1 Sam. 30:6).

But God has another way of renewing our strength, that is, when we "wait on [or hope in] the Lord (cf. Ps. 27:14; Isa. 40:31). This often means a period of rest, a change of pace—a time of prayer and study of the Scriptures. Many times our Savior did just this (Luke 5:16), usually right before some important task (Luke 6:12; 9:18, 28).

In the New Testament, this renewing of strength is called "grace" (James 4). The word has two important meanings. It describes an attitude of God toward sinning creatures ("unmerited favor" we often call it). But biblical grace also refers to a power God bestows on His people—an ability to do something they otherwise could not do. Of course, such a power is also undeserved. This is the grace God promised Paul when he was troubled with the thorn in the flesh (2 Cor. 12:8). Such a meaning is probably intended in the many salutations of the epistles: "Grace, mercy, and peace." It was the apostles' fervent wish that his readers receive fresh gifts of God's gracious power as they continued their pilgrimages. At the same time, this renewal of strength is a shield against indolence, laziness, and distraction.

After fighting his battles and finally securing the throne for himself and Solomon, David reviewed his life of struggle and spoke of God's many acts of kindness toward him (Ps. 18:1ff.; 144:2). No single word would suffice, as human language is too impoverished for expressing God's greatness. Word must be piled upon word to give God His due. It is interesting that both lists include "shield." As the Old Testament type of Messiah, David was singled out by Satan for his attacks. In the course of the battle, David was grievously wounded and often maligned. It can also be said of him that he was

> hard pressed on every side, but not crushed; perplexed, but not in despair; persecuted, but not abandoned; struck down, but not destroyed. (2 Cor. 4:8-9)

That David lived as long and as victoriously as he did was due to the Shield who protected him. David assures us also that

> He is a shield
>   for all who take refuge in him.
>   (Ps. 18:30)

10. Fire

One of my most vivid childhood experiences occurred as I stood across the street from a burning paint store. At one and the same time, I was both terrified and fascinated by the crackling flames and the searing heat as hundreds of gallons of oils and paints were consumed by fire before my eyes. Later on, some of us viewed with quiet wonder the shell that was once an attractive and well-kept place of business. Our curiosity attracted us at the same time that we were repelled by the charred remains. We learned that fire was something to be feared. We were also made aware of ceaseless, relentless energy, constantly changing form but ever the same.

Among the early experiences of the people of God are several encounters with fire in which God revealed both His concern for them and the powerful energy He would display in caring for them and in judging their enemies.

Genesis 15

Abraham is rightly known as a man of faith. He might with equal justice be called a man of upsets. Perhaps more than any other Old Testament saint, Abraham was shaken out of any set lifestyle he might have enjoyed by a series of God's providences.

God called Abraham from his native Ur and then made him a stranger in the land unconditionally promised to him. God also gave a child to Abraham and his wife when birth was unthinkable for them and then required Abraham to be prepared to give up that child as a burnt offering to Himself. For these upsetting experiences Abraham certainly needed faith!

Another of Abraham's early experiences is recorded in Genesis 15. In a vision God promised him the child Isaac, who was to be born years later. In addition, God predicted that from this one son a host of descendants would be born which would possess the land. Abraham needed some assurance that these promises would be fulfilled. So, as the vision continued, God told Abraham to provide animals and birds for a covenantal sacrifice. The animals were divided, their respective halves placed opposite each other. As Abraham slept, darkness descended, "thick and dreadful." And God spoke. "Know for certain" that Isaac's descendants would have to live in Egypt for four hundred years; Egypt would mistreat them and be punished for it; all this would happen after Abraham himself had died at an old age; and his descendants would return to take the land as a lasting possession. These revelations posed a real test for a man whose faith had already been tried. They signified that disruption would continue in Abraham's life and in the lives of his descendants.

But Abraham had asked, "How can I know?" (v. 8). God guaranteed these promises by revealing Himself as fire: "a smoking firepot with a blazing torch appeared and passed between the pieces" (v. 17). In the vision to Abraham, God was acting out a covenant ceremony in which the promisor would pass between pieces of sacrificial animals. If the promisor did not keep what he had promised, he could justly be treated as the animals through which he had passed. (This rather elaborate ceremony is not unlike what happens among children today when they say "Cross my heart and hope to die.") There was no inherent necessity for the sovereign Lord to take such an oath, but surely He was stooping to a human level to encourage His child, who needed all the encouragement he could get!

But in doing so, God appeared as a smoking firepot and a blazing torch! Why a symbol of fire? Almost any other symbol would have done just as well. Perhaps the fire encouraged and comforted Abraham by illustrating God's relentless energy that would be exercised in its proper time in behalf of Abraham and his descendants. And perhaps the torch strengthened Abraham as it shed its solitary light in the midst of the "thick and dreadful darkness."

It would take tremendous bursts of power to accomplish God's promises. As God destroyed the darkness of heathenism in Egypt and Canaan, the light afforded by the Abrahamic covenant would provide guidance for his descendants and a protective barrier against all enemies.

Exodus 3

All of us tend to seek a routine in life. Even after we have been disappointed in some plan and have to redirect our lives, we usually find comfort in a routine that brings stability and meaning. So it was with Moses. He had been brought up in Pharaoh's palace, perhaps with the expectation of power and influence. Probably he expected to use his position to the advantage of his people, Israel. But, as we know, those expectations were shattered, and at forty years of age Moses found himself an exile, a mere shepherd far from the court of Pharaoh. For forty more years he settled into a routine of Bedouin living, doubtless expecting that such an existence would be his until death.

And then, "the angel of the Lord appeared to him in flames of fire from within a bush" (v. 2). It was not the fire that initially attracted Moses, but the fact that "though the bush was on fire it did not burn up." As God "called to him from the midst of the bush," Moses learned that this was holy ground.

Once again God was using fire to reveal Himself. This revelation would disturb the complacency of one of the children God had chosen to fulfill the promises made to Abraham.

God might have used any strange thing to attract Moses' attention, but once again He chose fire as the emblem of His presence, a fire with the added distinction that it did not consume the bush. Did all this happen to remind Moses of Abraham's experience in Genesis 15? This is by no means a far-fetched question, since God introduced Himself (v. 6) as "the God of Abraham." Moses was probably taught the patriarchal stories by oral tradition or written word as Jochebed raised him for Pharaoh's daughter.

So, the fire Moses saw was not for destruction. It would sanctify Israel. Its ceaseless energy would protect Moses from the Egyptians, and it would direct him to the Land of Promise.

Exodus 13

The Israelites as a nation had ambivalent feelings about Egypt. On the one hand, it was a house of bondage and the people groaned under their hardships. Still, Egypt was home to them, the only home they had ever known, and the stability of its routines held its attractions (see Exod. 4:31; 5:20-23; 6:9; 14:11;16:3, and there are others). The Israelites also had conflicting feelings about the Exodus, about the forbidding desert they had to cross. A mixed multitude (12:38), they had vacillating feelings about Moses' God. Nevertheless, objectively at least, they were God's children and for that reason precious in His sight.

So when they were approaching the desert and ignorant that Pharaoh was plotting their destruction by a mighty army, God gave His people visible symbols of His presence: "By day the Lord went ahead of them in a pillar of cloud to guide them on their way and by night in a pillar of fire to give them light" (v. 21). The "pillar" was for guidance and encouragement, something that could be seen day and night.[1] This fiery manifestation was God's way of saying, "Here I am, as I promised Abraham and Moses. When I move, you will know that I am going ahead of you. When I stop, you can set up camp. Rest assured that I will be with you to protect you" (cf. Exod. 40:36-38).

The column of fire demonstrated this truth as Pharaoh and his army approached. The people cried out in unbelief, thinking that slavery in Egypt was to be preferred to being in the desert with God. Suddenly the pillar moved from the forward position of leading the people of God to a protective stance at the rear between themselves and Pharaoh. All night long, the Egyptians beheld a cloud of darkness while Israel enjoyed God's light. "In the morning watch God looked down from the pillar of fire and cloud at the Egyptian army and threw it into confusion" (14:24). Eventually, Pharaoh's army was destroyed in the sea. As Moses sang about this, he described the destruction as a sign of God's burning anger, which consumed the enemy like stubble (15:7). The promise to Abraham and Moses held true.

Exodus 19 and 24

At Sinai the people were faced with a temptation their forefathers never knew. They were to have God with them *all the time*, visibly present in the column of cloud and fire, symbolically present in the tabernacle soon to be erected. To have someone with you all the time can lead to taking that person for granted. But to take God for granted is grievous sin. So God's revelation of Himself took on an added dimension. When the elders of Israel saw a vision of God, "the glory of the Lord looked like a consuming fire" (24:17). On Sinai the fire had been combined with other terrifying symbols of God's presence—thunder and lightning, an earthquake, and a trumpet blast. But none of these frightened the people like the voice of God Himself (20:19). That voice proclaimed God as a jealous God, punishing sin and covenant breaking. And that jealousy was once and for all attached to the symbol of fire (Deut. 4:24).

The temptation to take God for granted and to ignore His holiness continued throughout the Bible. We need only mention the trespasses of Nadab and Abihu (Lev. 10), of Uzzah (2 Sam. 6), Uzziah (2 Chron. 26), Ananias and Sapphira (Acts 5), and the Corinthians who celebrated the Lord's Supper without recognizing the body of the Lord (1 Cor. 11:29f.). In these experiences the people saw the kindness and severity of God in His self-revealing emblems of fire. They were aware that these were not representations of static and abstract truths but were evidences of a continuing divine energy characteristic of an omnipotent God.

The Prophets

Later events in Israel's history were largely reminders of what the covenant fire symbolizes—God's power of judgment and of His protection. The fire that consumed Nadab and Abihu (Lev. 10) and the chariots of fire that protected Elisha at Dothan (2 Kings 6:17) are two examples.

With Isaiah, however, a new facet in God's self-revelation by fire appears. In chapter 6, the prophet saw a vision of the Lord in the temple, and he was struck with intense remorse because of his unclean lips. A seraph then touched those lips with a fiery coal from the altar, saying, "See, this has touched your lips; your guilt is taken away and your sin atoned for" (v. 7). The new element in the symbolism of fire—similar to the earlier meanings of consuming judgment and protecting power but an advance over them— was fire's purifying action. We see this even more clearly in Malachi 3. In speaking of the coming of "the messenger of the covenant," God said,

> He will be like a refiner's fire or a launderer's soap. He will sit as a refiner and purifier of silver; he will purify the Levites and refine them like gold and silver. (vv. 2, 3)

There is a similarity between the days of Isaiah and those of Malachi. Though some three hundred years separated these two ministries and a devastating exile in the interim brought judgment on the people for their transgressions, yet the attitude in Israel in both instances betrayed hypocrisy, formalism, and deceit. The two prophets were among "people of unclean lips," and their respective leaders were no better. Refining fire would be required before the nation could be a useful instrument for God's purposes.

In Isaiah's time the refining fire consisted of the exile and the events leading up to it. From its zenith of power as a nation under Uzziah and Jotham, Judah lost its prestige and even its land until the words of Isaiah were fulfilled:

> Until the cities lie ruined
>   and without inhabitant,
> until the houses are left deserted
>   and the fields ruined and ravaged,
> until the Lord has sent everyone far away
>   and the land is utterly forsaken.
>
> (6:11f.)

In Malachi's time, the refining fire loomed in the more distant future. The calamitous events of the intertestamental period and the preaching of John the Baptist were certainly part of this fire. The dross to be removed included sorcery, adultery, lying, defrauding workers of their wages, oppressing widows and orphans, and depriving aliens of justice. Yet all these social ills had a deeper root—the people did not truly fear the Lord Almighty (3:5).

Such ills were certainly not purged from the people of God at the time the New Testament was being written. Both James and Peter continued the metaphor of a purifying fire that perfects the saints for works of service (cf. James 1:2f., 12; 5:1-6; 1 Pet. 1:6-7; 4:12-19).

And while the refining work of God is surely within the human spirit, He used the persecutions of the first century as one of the instruments of that purification. Both apostles seem to allude to such events.

We have every reason to expect that God will continue the purifying of His saints until His coming again.

The New Testament

The crowning revelation of God as fire, one that gathers all the previous teaching into one harmonious whole, was the pentecostal experience of Acts 2:3. "They saw what seemed to be tongues of fire that separated and came to rest on each of them." This was the coming of the Holy Spirit, the baptism of fire predicted by John the Baptist and Jesus in the

Gospels. The Old Testament also had a symbol for this event.

The candelabra in the tabernacle may well have typified the Holy Spirit's presence. This view takes on added significance when we read in Zechariah 4 that the prophet's vision of a lighted lampstand was interpreted as a message to Zerubbabel, who would succeed in rebuilding the temple "'not by might, nor by power, but by my Spirit,' says the Lord Almighty." Later John saw what many take to be a vision of the heavenly temple. There he saw "before the throne, seven lamps blazing. These are the seven spirits of God" (Rev. 4:6). If these bits of data fit together, the Spirit was earlier symbolized by fire (as well as by oil) in the Holy Place of the Old Testament tabernacle.

In interpreting his own baptism as a preparatory rite, John the Baptist predicted that Jesus "would baptize with the Holy Spirit and fire" (Matt. 3:11). Although some suggest that the words "the Holy Spirit" refer to Pentecost and "fire" refers to a still future judgment, it is certainly consistent with Scripture to see both terms linked together (as a hendiadys) for the Spirit. Similarly, we should interpret Jesus' words, "I have come to bring fire on the earth, and how I wish it were already kindled" (Luke 12:49) to refer to Pentecost.[2] Jesus showed His disciples that this could not happen until He had suffered on the cross (v. 50).

Thus on Pentecost the Spirit was poured out as tongues of fire came to rest on each of those present. The fact that the fire did not burn the believers is reminiscent of the burning bush. And this event encouraged the disciples to believe that as He was with Moses so the Spirit would be with them in their founding of the holy nation, a people belonging to God.

Living as we do in the time of fulfillment, we should not expect shadows of things to come (Col. 2:17) or experiences with fire similar to those in the Old Testament. But the reality of which fire was the symbol should not be ignored for that reason. We must see with the eye of faith what is no longer symbolized.

The experience of Elisha and his servant may well have anticipated our day. The armies of the Aramite king had surrounded the city of Dothan, seeking to capture the prophet and

hale him before the king. Elisha was cool and confident, but his
servant was at wits' end.

> "Oh, my lord, what shall we do?" the servant asked. "Don't be
> afraid," the prophet answered. "Those who are with us are more
> than those who are with them." And Elisha prayed, "O Lord,
> open his eyes so he may see." Then the Lord opened the servant's
> eyes, and he looked and saw the hills full of horses and chariots
> of fire all around Elisha. (2 Kings 6:15-17)

Echoing Elisha's words, Paul wrote in Romans 8:31, "If God
is for us, who can be against us?" The reality has not changed
with the coming of the new age. The chariots of protecting fire
still surround the children of God!

Moreover, the fire symbolic of His holiness still attends us.
When we approach God in the temple of our hearts or in the
temple that is the congregation of the saints, we may miss the
mountain with its fire and smoke, the earthquake and trumpet
blast, or even the temple filled with smoke. But the God whose
name is jealous has lost none of His holiness or majesty. We can
only approach Him, in private or in public, with reverence and
godly fear.

Paul also spoke to the churches of the energy and power of the
Holy Spirit at work in the saints. It is the power shown in Christ's
resurrection—the power to conquer Satan, death, and sin (Eph.
1:19). It is the power that converted a sinner like Saul (3:7) and
makes the body of Christ a unity, thereby causing it to grow (4:16).
And it is the power in Paul's ministry to enable him to preach the
Gospel to every creature under heaven (Col. 1:23, 29).

This is Abraham's fire and Zerubbabel's fire. It is the Holy
Spirit fulfilling the Old Testament figure—and even surpassing
it.

Notes
[1] The same Hebrew word translated as "pillar" here is used for "pillars" in
the temple. Perhaps a more modern expression would be "a column of smoke
and a column of fire."
[2] I am here following the suggestion of Geldenhuys, *Commentary on the
Gospel of Luke* (NICNT), 366.

11. Water

On our back porch we have a potted shamrock. Its green leaves and white flowers brighten up the porch area during the summer days. But that same plant wilts when the soil is allowed to dry up. The leaves lose their luster, and the stalks droop. But a remarkable thing happens soon after the wilted plant is watered again. The slim stalks, bent over and limp, visibly regain their strength. Over a period of some minutes we watch the stalks raise themselves to their former height and beauty.

Just as the plant world thrives on water, so the animal and human species depend on it. Pictures of the recent drought in Africa have brought home to us the extremely debilitating effects a lack of water has on all living creatures. It was no different in biblical times. Joel describes the effect of drought on cattle:

> How the cattle moan!
>> The herds mill about
> because they have no pasture;
>> even the flocks of sheep are suffering.
>>>> (1:18)

David, too, knew the agonies of thirst when he was in the desert of Judah:

> O God, you are my God,
>   earnestly I seek you;
> my soul thirsts for you,
>   my body longs for you,
> in a dry and weary land
>   where there is no water.
>
> (Ps. 63:1)

The need for water was often on the minds of Israelites. Famines drove the patriarchs from the land (Gen. 12:10; 26:1ff.; 42:1ff.). Isaac had disputes with Abimelech's people regarding the use of wells. Beersheba ("the well of the oath") became Abraham's home because of the ample supply of water there.

In Canaan, cities were located near water supplies, and many areas received their names from wells or springs nearby: En-gedi, En-rogel, En-rimmon, to name a few (*en* is a transliteration of the Hebrew word for "well" or "spring").

Later on, when the nation was divided, the water supply for a city under siege became a paramount concern. Ahaz went out to inspect the aqueduct when he feared an attack by Israel and Syria (something of what he wanted to avoid can be gleaned from 2 Kings 6:24f.). Hezekiah's celebrated tunnel by which he brought water into Jerusalem was constructed out of concern for water in case of attack.

Occasional droughts reminded the Israelites of their dependence on water, and such times were seen as judgments of God for the nation's departures from the law. Solomon saw fit to include a petition for rain in his prayer of dedicating the temple. Significantly, God responded:

> I have heard your prayer.... When I shut up the heavens so that there is no rain ... if my people, who are called by my name, will humble themselves and pray and seek my face and turn from their wicked ways, then I will hear from heaven and will forgive their sin and heal their land. (2 Chron. 7:12-14)

Thus their own experiences taught the people about their total dependence on God for life-sustaining water. And they were not allowed to forget one of the earliest lessons God taught them, at Meribah, when the people were given water to drink from the rock (Exod. 17:1-7; cf. Num. 20:1-13). That story is referred to again and again throughout the Bible (Deut. 8:15; Ps. 78:15f.; Isa. 43:20; 48:21; 1 Cor. 10:4). The event is a great Old Testament example of grace (God's unmerited favor). Even though the Israelites had grumbled against God and doubted His love and care, He gave them the water they craved in such abundance that they and their livestock were fully satisfied.

To teach His people their dependence on Him, God uses the image of water in two figures of speech. First, He *gives* living water; second, He *is* the water of life. We shall study only the second of these since this is a figurative expression of God Himself. The overall lesson of this chapter is well expressed by John Calvin: "As it was the spiritual life of Adam to remain united and bound to his Maker, so estrangement from him was the death of his soul."[1] It is only by virtue of our union with God, the water of life, that we live. When we choose to ignore Him and His claims upon us, we are dead.

Hosea 14

Chapter 14 in Hosea is one of the clearest expressions of sovereign grace in the Scriptures. For thirteen chapters the Lord had condemned the infidelity, lukewarmness, and idolatry of the nation of Israel and had promised its destruction within a few years. The mood then changed to one of forgiveness, repentance, and restoration.

The prophet began with an exhortation to the nation to return to God, pointing out two truths obvious by now. First, God's people were suffering not because they were weak but because they had turned from God. Second, their assurance that Assyria would deliver them and their confidence that Baal would promote their prosperity were based on empty hopes indeed.

So Hosea counseled the people to return to the Lord and,

after due confession of their iniquities, to ask Him for His gracious help. Destitute as they were, they could find some comfort in the words "for in you the fatherless find compassion" (v. 3).

Heretofore Israel had made some sort of confession, but it was shallow and unaccompanied with any sort of change in the life of the nation. Now there would be reformation: "receive us graciously, that we may offer the fruit of our lips" (v. 2). As the *Anchor Bible* puts it, "Fruit of lips must mean the vows and promises made, including not only offerings but commitment in worship and service."[2] Hebrews 13:15 may well be a citation of Hosea's passage:

> Through Jesus, therefore, let us continually offer to God a sacrifice of praise—the fruit of lips that confess his name. And do not forget to do good and to share with others, for with such sacrifices God is pleased. (vv. 15-16)

Here is clear evidence that good works can only follow the work of God's grace in our hearts. Good works have no merit in themselves; rather, they are an expression of thanks given by those who have experienced God's love despite the revolting character of their sin. The penitents in Hosea 14 intend to be careful to maintain good works.

God's response is recorded in verses 5 and following. Hosea marshalls his very impressive rhetorical powers in eight comparisons (similes) to express the fullness of divine grace and its power in the lives of penitents. God's favor and its effects are like *dew*, like a *lily*, like a *cedar*, like an *olive tree*, like the *grain*, like a *vine*, and like *wine*.

The effects of God's grace are described in terms taken from the world of plants. Since the significance of some of these similes may be obscure to us living so many years later, a few words of comment may be called for.

"Like dew." God Himself, the source of all grace, is likened to dew. In the Book of Hosea, dew has two basic characteristics. The morning dew is ephemeral and soon gone; this describes Israel's professed love and fidelity to God (see 6:4; 13:3). But dew

also has a good purpose; it provides much-needed moisture and makes the difference, in some climates, between barrenness and lush growth. In response to Israel's call for forgiveness and acceptance, God will visit the land like dew, and the vegetation will abound.

Note His words in verse 4: "[I] will love them freely." What is given freely is usually also given generously, and the similes show how richly God's grace meets the needs of His people.

"Like a lily." Keil quotes from Pliny's *Natural History:* "[the lily] is unsurpassed in its fecundity, often producing fifty bulbs from a single root."[3]

"Like a cedar." The deep roots of the tree provide stability and insure a steady source of nutriment. Thus supplied, the branches proliferate. The aroma from the cedar is a deterrent to pests and diseases.

"Like an olive tree." "The Jews were pictured as olive trees, for they were to yield 'fruits' where other trees could not grow."[4]

"Like the grain." "Yielding a hundred, sixty, or thirty times what was sown" (Matt. 13:23).

"Like a vine." Perhaps a reference to Genesis 49:22:

> Joseph is a fruitful vine,
>   a fruitful vine near a spring,
>   whose branches climb over a wall.

"Like the wine from Lebanon." Again Keil quotes Pliny as evidence that "the wine from Lebanon has been celebrated from time immemorial."[5]

These similes suggest a people so blessed by God's grace that they multiply rapidly—thriving where other peoples cannot, solidly established so as to be unaffected by changes in the world, able to preserve themselves from contamination, and enjoying a worldwide reputation as a people favored by God. This is the heritage of the church. During periods of her revival, these blessings are enjoyed in abundance. United to God and enjoying His life-giving power, the saints bear the fruit of the Spirit to an unparalleled degree. But during times of decline, these figures of speech stand as a rebuke to lukewarm believers. And they hold out a promise to be fulfilled upon repentance and renewal.

We should not forget the Giver by being too much taken up with the gifts. The recital of the effects of the dew upon Israel is meant to demonstrate that "your fruitfulness comes from me" (v. 8).

Jeremiah 2:13; 17:13

But years after Hosea's message, Jeremiah was to rebuke the southern kingdom, Judah, for this sin—forgetting the very one from whom their blessings came. We may not be sure whether Hosea's words were read in Judah, but surely the truth of those words had been spoken by the prophets all the way back to Moses. Just as Hosea detailed the blessings of a fresh water supply, so Jeremiah described what would happen when people turn away from a source of water.

Jeremiah understood Israel's history as few of his contemporaries did. As he reviewed their past in chapter 2, he recalled their earlier devotion to the Lord and the holiness which came from that devotion. The nation was "the first fruits of his harvest; all who devoured her were held guilty, and disaster overtook them" (v. 3).

But the nation soon forgot those days and did not realize the source of their blessings. For some years, Judah had been a vassal state, depending for its life and continuance on Egypt and Assyria. But why should God's people, "the first fruits of his harvest" (v. 3), ever be vassals to anyone? Clearly, there was no rational explanation for such conduct, except that the people preferred it that way. God censured them for this. In fact, He said that what they were doing had no parallel among the nations of the time (vv. 5-11). Heathen nations did not change their gods so easily! Then echoing the words of Moses (Deut. 32:1), He invoked the heavens to show their horror at such deeds.

His analysis of Judah's crime was straightforward enough:

> My people have committed two sins:
> They have forsaken me,
>   the spring of living water,

and have dug their own cisterns,
    broken cisterns that cannot hold water.
                    (2:13)

The choice confronting people in the world is between water
and no water. Water produces results, some of which are depicted
for us by Hosea—results found in the Lord and only in Him.
Lack of water produces thirst—and then death. There is no
middle ground.

Yet the deceitfulness of sin is seen most clearly in the fact that
people persist in seeking that middle ground, which does not
exist. They persist in looking for water where none can be found.
Note God's words:

Now why go to Egypt
    to drink water from the Shihor [a demeaning reference to the
        Nile]?
And why go to Assyria
    to drink water from the River [the Euphrates]?
                    (2:18)

Here was a people whose history was rich in instances of
God's deliverance from nations large and small and whose
prophets had constantly advised their kings that safety lay in
obedience to God and trust in His promises. Yet in their perversity, the Jews continued to prefer treaties with other nations
and their gods as the source of their national identity and
prosperity. Their plan would not work for three reasons. First,
the nations in whom they were trusting were broken cisterns,
able to hold no water (v. 36). Second, those very nations from
whom they were seeking help would turn upon them and
deplete their resources (v. 16). Third, Judah would have to face
up to the righteous providence of God, who would bring
disaster on it and the nations to whom it had appealed. The
people of God would have occasion to say, "If only we had not
forsaken God!"

In chapter 17, Jeremiah returned to his quarrel with Jerusalem for forsaking the spring of living water (v. 13). The first part

of the chapter renewed the threat of judgment and added the promise of blessing.

God would not stand idly by while the nation rushed after false gods and pagan nations. In due time, Judah would be plundered (v. 3) and lose its inheritance and be enslaved to its enemies (v. 4). Forgetting that He is a jealous God, the people had kindled God's everlasting anger.

Within a few years, Judah, which once blossomed as the Garden of Eden, would be "like a bush in the wastelands . . . he will dwell in the parched places of the desert, in a salt land where no one lives." If any good thing is happening (Oswalt suggests this might refer to rain),[6] it will pass by Judah. Since the nation has chosen to have no water, no water will it have.

It is frightening to contemplate the doom of those in our day who pride themselves in their humanism, content to rest their own hopes, as well as the hopes of the world, on scientific knowledge alone. Perhaps only a few believe this way explicitly (e.g., the signers of first and second *Humanist Manifestos*), but they have a host of devoted followers who refuse the spring of living water. Their future? "Those who turn away from you will be written in the dust," and desert winds will obliterate every memory of them.

There are, however, those who do not refuse to drink. They trust in the Lord and have confidence in Him. This reference defines for us what it is to drink the living water. Those who do so are like trees planted by water (here Jeremiah is clearly referring to, and enlarging upon, Psalm 1). Because the tree "sends out its roots by the stream":

> It does not fear when heat comes;
>   its leaves are always green.
> It has no worries in a year of drought
>   and never fails to bear fruit.

(17:8)

God has not promised us permanent relief from heat or drought, but He has promised that living water will be available to those who have confidence in Him. And in the life to come they will find that their names, from all eternity, have been written in the Lamb's Book of Life (Rev. 13:8). What a contrast between the names written in sand and those written in God's Book!

Notes
[1] *Institutes of the Christian Religion*, trans. Battles, 1:246.
[2] Andersen and Freedman, *Hosea*, 645.
[3] *Minor Prophets*, 1:165.
[4] ZPEB, 4:528.
[5] *Minor Prophets*, 1.
[6] *Book of Isaiah, 1-39* (NICOT), 420.

12. Light

The scene might be multiplied thousands of times in homes across the land, even around the world. It is bedtime. The child is sleepy enough, but there is one problem. She wants a light left on in the room. The darkness is scary, and a light would be reassuring. She would be asleep in a moment if only a light could stay on!

Why is light so comforting, and darkness such a cause for fear? There seems to be an instinctive understanding in many cultures that light is good and beautiful, that it signifies the truth. Darkness represents evil, the ugly and false. In our day historians speak of the Enlightenment as a time when there was a renaissance not only of knowledge but also of freedom and progress. The Dark Ages describe a period of ignorance, slavery, and backwardness.

Jesus, however, warns us that this natural instinct regarding light and darkness has been perverted. In the Sermon on the Mount He described the eye as the "lamp of the body." When our eyes are acting properly they give good and true information to the rest of the body. So, if a rock lies in our pathway and we see it clearly, we use our hands and feet to get around it and thus prevent injury. But our eyes may be faulty and unable to see the obstacle in our path. And those same hands and feet may even be injured when we strike the unseen rock. As a result, what we thought was light is for all practical purposes darkness—and "how great is that darkness!" (Matt. 6:22f.) So our natural instinct may confuse what is light and safe with what is darkness and dangerous. We certainly need help in determining which is the true light.

In Matthew 6 it is easy to see what Jesus was calling darkness. True darkness is manifested in the hypocrisy of doing things so that others will think us holy and in trusting that their estimate of us is an accurate description of who we are (vv. 1-18); in trusting in earthly riches as though there is no life after death (vv. 19-25); and in being overly concerned with the affairs and demands of this life as though we had to fulfill them without God's help (vv. 25-34). So Jesus, early in His ministry, turned the searchlight of God on sins common to all of us, sins that block out the knowledge of God. When we see such sins as stumbling blocks, we may turn from them; if we see them as trinkets to be treasured, we are already floundering in the darkness.

This is why Jesus, in His capacity as Messiah, is called "the true light that gives light to every man" (John 1:9). The word "true" here might also be translated "genuine" or "authentic" in contrast to those so-called lights that are really darkness and lead people astray and into destruction.

The Bible frequently contrasts light with darkness. Westcott gives us some idea of how "light" and "darkness" are used.[1]

Light	Darkness
•truth	•falsehood
•good	•evil
•joy	•sorrow
•safety	•peril
•life	•death

The strongest contrasts between light and darkness are found in the writings of John.

1 John 1

In the first chapter of 1 John, God is seen in His holiness. John's purpose in his preaching, and perhaps in writing this letter, was to tell what the apostles saw and heard. As a result, the hearers and readers might have fellowship ("something in common") with other saints of the time, and with the Father and Son as well. One of the things they heard was that "God is light; in him there is no darkness at all."

In making this assertion, the apostle may be referring to John 3:19 and following, where the effects of light and darkness upon people are contrasted. Light (i.e., Jesus) has come into the world. But men hate Him and will not come to Him, because they love darkness and do evil. Therefore they do not want their deeds exposed. Such hardened sinners must not be confused with those who repent and turn to Jesus, for hardened sinners continually love evil and prefer it to God's deliverance. His condemnation already rests on such people who reject the Light.

John was stressing the absolute antithesis between light and darkness. That is why he continued, ". . . in him there is no darkness at all." Many things in this world are by their nature relative, but the contrast between God and evil is absolute indeed.

Because this is so, it is inconsistent for people to walk in darkness and still claim to have something in common with God. Their lives become a lie—they "do not live by the truth." This is a warning to those who feel they can continue in sin because they have been saved by grace. Their doctrine is sometimes called "cheap grace" and "carnal security." But by whatever name it is known, such a doctrine is condemned throughout Scripture. Grace never contradicts holiness. In fact, grace begets holiness in the life of a regenerated person.

As John continued his discussion, it is evident that light is being set forth in ethical terms. We are not speculating about the nature of light, but God is revealing Himself in holiness, purity, and power, which are characteristics of light.

Therefore, walking in the light has an assured effect: saints will have fellowship with each other (in 1 John such activity is always a proof of fellowship with God; see 2:9-11; 3:14, 17). Living according to God brings unity among the people of God, because the light first reveals every kind of error and then purifies it. Light unifies by helping us see ourselves as we really are. For example, in a dark room, a woman wearing a red dress and another woman wearing a blue dress may think their colors are identical, but light will reveal the difference. If they want color harmony, one (or both) has to change dresses. So it is in the church. Paul's appeal to unity among the Philippians is based on the light of God's truth. Euodia and Syntyche (and the rest of the church) may well contemplate the significance of the Incarnation so that they may give up their petty differences.

This is a call for Bible reading with a particular personal application. We must read with a willingness to see ourselves as we really are ("to come to the light") and to be ready to change in order to have things in common with others in the body.

The metaphor of light alone is insufficient to express the whole scope of salvation. Light, in John's day, was not known for its cleansing and curative effects (he did not, for example, know of laser beams). So in addition to the light, he must speak of the blood of Jesus, which purifies us from every sin (v. 7). So wonderfully meritorious is the sacrifice of Christ that every sin of every Christian has been declared forgiven. We are justified in God's sight.

Even so, we may not claim to be sinless in our day-to-day living, for that would make Him a liar and show that we are not following the Word. True walking in the light recognizes the reality of sin in all of us and, therefore, entails confession on our part (v. 9) and intercession on the part of the assembly of believers (2:1). Individual confession, because of Christ's merit, brings forgiveness and an immediate renewal of fellowship.

However, walking in the light is not an individual responsibility only; it is the responsibility of all of us. Part of walking in the light is to love and restore an erring brother and sister.

It is a beautiful thing when the Gospel is compared with the darkness of those beliefs which are not really gospels at all. It speaks of God who is pure "light," absolutely holy. The Gospel speaks of the benevolent and beneficent rays of the message He has brought into the world. People come to Him as to light. They are united with others who walk according to it, and they are prepared for the day of even greater light when the last wisps of darkness pass away.

Psalm 27

In Psalm 27 God is seen as the protector of His saints, and His promises are the basis for their hope. David called the Lord his "light" as well as his "salvation" and the "stronghold of his life." These words, because of the parallelism of Hebrew poetry, are probably synonyms; that is, "salvation" and "stronghold" help us define "light." For David, "light" meant protection. Therefore, he was not afraid of evil men, his enemies, or even an army that might oppose him. When they attack, they will only stumble and fall. In what did David put his confidence?

In the second stanza of the psalm, David spoke of a single desire in his heart—"that I may dwell in the house of the Lord all the days of my life." He went on to describe the tabernacle as a shelter from trouble and enemies. Dahood suggests that this is a reference to eternal life and David's desire to be with the Lord. However, the psalmist mentions "trouble" and "enemies" (vv. 5-6), and these elements are clearly out of place in heaven.

So David was speaking of his *present* experiences. In earlier chapters we followed the ups and downs of David's career (cf. chaps. 7, 8). Therefore we know something of the trouble he had throughout his life. Calvin may be right when he taught that the psalmist was writing this meditation during one of his exiles. David's heart was back in Jerusalem, where the ark resided in a tent. If only he could be there to see the ark, reflect on its significance, "to gaze upon the beauty of the Lord!" There David knew he would be safe not because the ark was some sort of relic with magic powers (the nation had learned that lesson; 1 Sam. 4) but because he could take refuge in what the ark signified—the deliverance from all evil.

What David did in his day was an example for us living this side of the Cross. God no longer lives within a tabernacle but dwells within us and in the church. In another context Jesus appears in the tabernacle in heaven and there intercedes for our protection from all kinds of evil. When we reflect on those truths, and when we contemplate the sacraments He instituted for our help and encouragement, we are able to repeat with even greater understanding,

> The Lord is my light and salvation—
> whom shall I fear?

(v. 1)

What was true of David could also be said of the nation. Light would appear in Judah's future to give protection and hope. Isaiah saw the coming of the Assyrian nation to be the rod of God's anger against Judah and Jerusalem. The Assyrians would accomplish all of God's purpose but with such pride and arrogance that God would bring an appropriate judgment upon that whole nation (10:5-16):

> Therefore, the Lord, the Lord Almighty,
>   will send a wasting disease upon his [Assyria's] sturdy warriors;
> under his pomp a fire will be kindled
>   like a blazing flame.

(10:16)

That blazing flame would be the Lord Himself:

> The Light of Israel will become a fire,
>   their Holy One a flame.

(10:17)

It may well be that Isaiah was recalling the Light that protected Israel during the time of the Exodus, the wall of fire that delivered Israel from the Egyptians by sending them into the Red Sea. That same Light would appear again in behalf of the nation and in a different judgment deliver them from the Assyrians.

Isaiah's contemporary, Micah, inveighed against the northern nation:

> You have observed the statues of Omri
>   and all the practices of Ahab's house,
>   and you have followed their traditions.

> Therefore I will give you over to ruin
>   and your people to derision;
>   you will bear the scorn of nations.
>
>   (6:16)

Yet the covenant-keeping God will not judge His people forever:

> Though I sit in darkness,
>   the Lord will be my light. . . .
> He will bring me out into the light;
>   I will see his [justice].
>
>   (7:8-9)

As Micah viewed the nation's plight, he saw hope in the grace of God. Calvin suggests the following interpretation: "As when one is cast into a deep pit, by raising upward his eyes, he sees at a distance the light of the sun; so also the obscure and thick darkness of tribulations may not so far prevail as to shut out from us every spark of light, and to prevent faith from raising our eyes upward, that we may taste some of God's goodness."[2] It is important to note that when the Lord fulfills this word, He will do it according to the principles of justice. When God blesses His chosen people, no one will be able to question what He has done. We are reminded of Paul's words:

> Who will bring any charge against those whom God has chosen? It is God who justifies. (Rom. 8:33)

Clearly, when God reveals Himself as light, He wants us to take hope in His promises of protection and favor.

In their visions of the distant future, the prophets of both the Old and New Testaments saw a most extraordinary thing. The sun and moon are no longer needed in the New Heavens:

> for the Lord will be your everlasting light,
>   and your God will be your glory.
> Your sun will never set again,
>   and your moon will wane no more;
> the Lord will be your everlasting light,
>   and your days of sorrow will end.
>   (Isa. 60:19-20; cf. Rev. 21:23; 22:5)

This vision of the future gathers together all the aspects of God as light. In the holiness of heaven there will be no sorrow; there will be nothing to vie with the Lord for first place in the hearts of the redeemed. The vision of eternal light comes to a people "forsaken and hated" (Isa. 60:15). And this vision of heaven stands as a blessed hope for all those who have come to the Light.

Notes
[1] *The Epistles of St. John*, 17. The passages here summarized are Matt. 4:16; Luke 1:79; 11:35f.; John 3:19, 20; 1 Pet. 2:9; 2 Cor. 4:6; 6:14; Ps. 27:1.
[2] *Commentaries on the Twelve Minor Prophets*, 3:375.

Part Three

Animals
as
Mirrors of His Glory

13. Moth

One of my earliest recollections from childhood has to do with a moth and the excitement caused in our home by its presence in one of our clothes closets. The discovery of that moth caused much disgust and chagrin among the adult members in our family. And immediate attempts were made to deal with the pest and any eggs it might have laid. Moths are certainly not the most favorite of creatures. Why, then, would God call Himself a moth, of all things?

> I am like a moth to Ephraim,
> like rot to the people of Judah.
>
> (Hos. 5:12)

If we know something about the people Hosea was addressing and the events taking place in the eighth century before Christ, we will understand why God chose this particular metaphor.

Jeroboam II was king over Israel (the northern kingdom) when Hosea began his prophetic ministry. Jeroboam was the most successful of the descendants of Jehu, ruling when neighboring powers were weak or occupied elsewhere.

Whereas under his predecessors there had been a continual loss of territory and prestige, he recaptured what had been lost to Israel's enemies "from Lebo Hamath to the Sea of Arabah" (what we today would call Jordan and part of Syria). The people had peace and prosperity during his forty-one-year reign—peace because for a change other nations posed no threat, prosperity because that peace fostered free trade.

A spirit of optimism gripped the people and, ironically, so did an expectation that God would once again keep His promises and Israel would recover the greatness enjoyed under Solomon. They were selective in what they believed and in what they ignored, but these Israelites were not pagans or atheists. On one hand, they could recall the ministries of Elijah and Elisha and remember what Jehu had done to the worship of Baal. On the other, they looked to Jeroboam II to keep the peace so they could enjoy themselves.

In their prosperity God's people built large and ornate buildings in which they gave themselves over to self-indulgence and complacency. Listen to Amos, a contemporary of Hosea:

> You lie on beds inlaid with ivory
> and lounge on your couches.
> You dine on choice lambs
> and fattened calves.
> You strum away on your harps like David
> and improvise on musical instruments.
> You drink wine by the bowlful
> and use the finest lotions. . . .
>
> (6:4-6)

They compounded these grievances by oppressing and ignoring the poor:

> They sell the righteous for silver,
> and the needy for a pair of sandals.
>
> (2:6)

> Hear this word, you cows of Bashan on Mount Samaria,
>> you women who oppress the poor and crush the needy
>> and say to your husbands, "Bring us some drinks!"
>>> (4:1)

It became dangerous to walk the streets at night:

> As marauders lie in ambush for a man,
>> so do bands of priests;
> they murder on the road to Shechem,
>> committing shameful crimes.
>>> (Hos. 6:9)

> They practice deceit,
>> thieves break into houses,
>> bandits rob in the streets.
>>> (7:1)

Faithfulness in civic matters had now become a thing of the past:

> They delight the king with their wickedness,
>> the princes with their lies.
>>> (Hos. 7:3)

> They make many promises,
>> take false oaths
>> and make agreements;
> therefore lawsuits spring up
>> like poisonous weeds in a plowed field.
>>> (10:4)

Amos finished his complaint above with the remark "... but you do not grieve over the ruin of Joseph" (6:6). How far Israel, the descendants of Joseph, had fallen from the greatness and dignity of that patriarch whom God has brought to the pinnacle of power in Egypt. They were so bent on pleasure that they took no thought, gave no time to think, of the evil gnawing away at their vitals.

Israel was ruined but did not know it. The people did not know that a moth had laid its eggs and the larvae were at work in the very fabric of their society. They did not know this because their own military power, great affluence, and peace with their neighbors blinded them to the truth. And then, too, they were very religious. In our reading of Hosea and his contemporary, Amos, we find no lack of zeal for festivals and sacrifices; prophets and priests were popular and influential figures in high places. Clearly in the minds of these people, their prosperity was due to the blessings of God—and only greater blessings lay in their future.

Such an attitude was reinforced by false prophets who knew what the people wanted to hear, and they preached it!

As Jeremiah would later describe their ilk:

> They dress the wound of my people
>   as though it were not serious.
> "Peace, peace," they say,
>   when there is no peace.
>
> (6:14; cf. 8:11)

But Hosea had a word from the Lord:

> Hear the word of the Lord, you Israelites,
>   because the Lord has a charge to bring
>   against you who live in the land:
> "There is no faithfulness, no love,
>   no acknowledgment of God in the land....
> Because of this the land mourns,
>   and all who live in it waste away;
> the beasts of the field and the birds of the air
>   and the fish of the sea are dying.
>
> (4:1-3)

Even as Hosea spoke, God was sending a drought upon Israel because of the sins mentioned. The slow, enervating, and degrading effect of a drought would have a result similar to larvae's destructive activity.

But in addition to agricultural and economic problems, political difficulties appeared both within and outside of the kingdom. An overview of Israel's history shows this:

King	Length of Reign	How Removed	Significant Events
Zechariah	6 months	Killed by Shallum.	
Shallum	1 month	Killed by Menahem.	
Menahem	10 years	Died.	Invaded by Assyria; tribute exacted of the wealthy.
Pekahiah	2 years	Killed by Pekah.	
Pekah	20 years	Killed by Hoshea.	Invaded by Assyria; land confiscated; people deported.
Hoshea	9 years	Deported.	Invaded by Assyria; 3-yr. siege.

After the reign of Jeroboam II, Israel had six kings who ruled a total of some 41 years. To call such men "kings" is a euphemism; they were vassals of the kings of Assyria and drained off the wealth of their country to keep up the semblance of reigning. But Assyria could not, or would not, protect them from their own countrymen, who thought nothing of murder and usurping the throne. The moth had laid the larvae of destruction during the reign of Jeroboam, as Hosea had said. The vitality and power of the country was short-lived and eventually destroyed.

The lesson in all this should be clear. Many people wait for evidence of judgment before they repent, but if the moth has done its work, the evidence comes too late, for the damage is already done.

Delitzsch, commenting on Isaiah 50:9 and 51:8, writes:

> They fall to pieces like a worn-out garment, and fall a prey to the moth which they already carry within them: [the figure] although apparently insignificant, is yet really a terrible one, inasmuch as it points to a power of destruction working imperceptibly and slowly, but yet effecting the destruction of the object selected with all the greater certainty. . . . the smallest exertion of strength is quite sufficient to annihilate their sham greatness and sham

power; and that long before they are actually destroyed, they carry the constantly increasing germ of it within themselves.[1]

The language Delitzsch uses is frightening, but it accurately describes the events. God, as moth, is just as powerful as God the lion or the leopard. And the destruction, though slow in coming, is just as effective. If only Israel had listened to Hosea!

It does not take great prophetic insight to see that many parallels exist between ancient Israel and the Western world today. Not only are the transgressions strikingly similar, the results of the larvae's working are also evident. Although the Western nations are not covenant people as Israel was, we have no reason to believe that we shall be neglected in the judgment of the Moth.

Notes
[1] Keil and Delitzsch, *The Prophecies of Isaiah*, 2:279f., 287.

14. Wild Beast

Hosea loved to use metaphors. He referred to Ephraim as cows (4:16), a pancake (7:8), and doves (7:11). Through the prophet God described Himself as a lion, a leopard, and a bear (13:7f.). In much of the world's literature, the lion is considered a noble beast symbolizing dignity (see Prov. 30:29f.), and the leopard and bear come in for their share of admiration, too. But as wild animals, lions, leopards, and bears also excite abject fear. Is God as terrifying as a wild beast?

In the next chapter, we shall see God's frightening power exhibited against the enemies of the saints. But does He ever direct that fury against His own people? Hosea's words present that alarming prospect.

Job had thought that God's treatment of him was like a wild beast's attack:

> If I hold my head high, you stalk me like a lion. . . .
> God assails me and tears me in his anger
> and gnashes his teeth at me.
> (10:16; 16:9)

As Job worked through his troubles, the greatest of which were mental and not physical, the great saint mistakenly ascribed them to God's wrath. Job did not realize that he had been chosen

115

to suffer because he was dear in the sight of God. Until the revelation of God's goodness, Job could only think of his Lord as a ravenous beast intent on his personal destruction.

What Job in his ignorance thought to be true was exactly what God promised to those who forget Him. Psalm 50 has an application to all the earth, but its message is especially to Israel; it is a description of judgment in fulfillment of His covenant. After pointing out the spiritual nature of the commandments, God turned to hypocrites who treated those commandments with disdain. Yes, He would act like a wild beast toward them. He promised them, "I will tear you to pieces, with none to rescue" (v. 22). This is a general principle for God's judgment upon those who forget Him, those who hate His instruction and cast His words behind them (see v. 17). These people are acquainted with His ways but choose, instead, to believe that He is altogether like them, that is, casual about His commands and the judgment that lies ahead. They are lulled into complacency by the thought "It can't happen to me."

Hosea took this general principle and made it a specific prophecy to be fulfilled in the near future if Israel continued in its hypocritical ways. After the moth prophecy (Hos. 5:12), which we studied in the previous chapter, the Lord says:

> For I will be like a lion to Ephraim,
>   like a great lion to Judah.
> I will tear them to pieces and go away;
>   I will carry them off, with no one to rescue them.
>   (Hos. 5:14)

(Note the language similar to Ps. 50:22.)

He repeats the threat with even greater vividness:

> So I will come upon them like a lion,
>   like a leopard I will lurk by the path.
> Like a bear robbed of her cubs,
>   I will attack them and rip them open.
> Like a lion I will devour them;
>   a wild animal will tear them apart.
>   (13:7f.)

What Hosea foresaw as happening to each part of the divided kingdom in its turn, Jeremiah predicted would happen in Judah, a nation that did not profit by Ephraim's example:

> Hear the cry of the shepherds, . . .
>   for the Lord is destroying their pasture. . . .
> Like a lion he will leave his lair,
>   and their land will become desolate
> because of the sword of the oppressor
>   and because of the Lord's fierce anger.
>   (25:36ff.)

We may be tempted to pass this off as mere imagery. Yes, imagery it may be, but it is also a picture of just what the writer of Lamentations himself experienced. In the midst of his affliction, the prophet wrote:

> Like a bear lying in wait,
>   like a lion in hiding,
> he dragged me from the path and mangled me
>   and left me without help.
>   (3:10)

One would have to read the entire Book of Lamentations to fill in the details of the Babylonian destruction of Jerusalem. It is expressed prosaically by the chronicler:

> He brought up against them the king of the Babylonians, who killed their young men with the sword in the sanctuary, and spared neither young man nor young woman, old man or aged. . . . He carried into exile to Babylon the remnant, who escaped from the sword, and they became servants to him and his sons until the kingdom of Persia came to power. (2 Chron. 36:17ff.)

Although the massacre and subsequent exile were terrifying beyond words, these calamities were, nevertheless, nothing more than had been predicted by Asaph in Psalm 50 and by the prophet Hosea. In fact, one may go back to Leviticus 26 and Deuteronomy 28 for even earlier prophecies regarding the consequences to Israel if the people did not keep the covenant. In the midst of his agony, Jeremiah could say with great truth,

> The Lord has done what he planned;
>> he has fulfilled his word
>> which he decreed long ago.
>>> (Lam. 2:17)

If Israel's experiences teach us anything, we should remember that God is "watching to see that my word is fulfilled" (Jer. 1:12). Just as this truth would have applied to the blessings of the covenant (Lev. 26:1-13; Deut. 28:1-14), so it promises blessings to all those who put their trust in Him. Equally, just as God's promises lamentably applied to the curses of the covenant (Lev. 26:14ff.; Deut. 28:15ff.), so should they send a chilling warning to all those who take lightly the words of the New Testament.

> Do not be deceived: God cannot be mocked. A man reaps what he sows. (Gal. 6:7)

> Let no one deceive you with empty words, for because of such things [immorality, greed, foolish talk] God's wrath comes on those who are disobedient. (Eph. 5:6)

There is another, and happier, side to this figure of speech. The vehemence with which God judges the hypocrites among His people can also be directed against those who hate Zion and its inhabitants:

> As a lion growls,
>> a great lion over his prey . . .
> so the Lord Almighty will come down
>> to do battle on Mount Zion and on its heights
>>> (Isa. 31:4)

Isaiah went on to describe how the Assyrian menace would be dealt with. First, he predicted the outcome in chapter 31, then he described the fall of Sennacherib's army in chapter 37.

Chapter 31	*Chapter 37*
Assyria will fall by a sword that is not of man. (v. 8)	Then the angel of the Lord went out and put to death a hundred and eighty-five thousand men in the Assyrian camp. (v. 36)

This, in literal terms, was the result of the Lion's growling over His prey. The savagery and extent of the destruction came in answer to Hezekiah's prayer recorded in Isaiah 37:15-17, 20. It is a model plea for every Christian in danger from the Lord's enemies:

> O Lord Almighty, God of Israel, enthroned between the cheru-bim, you alone are God over all the kingdoms of the earth. You have made heaven and earth. Give ear, O Lord, and hear; open your eyes, O Lord, and see; listen to all the words Sennacherib has sent to insult the living God. . . .
> Now, O Lord our God, deliver us from his hand, so that all kingdoms on earth may know that you alone, O Lord, are God.

In earlier chapters we have seen evidences of God's love for His people portrayed by other metaphors. Here is an insight into the violence of His concern for the welfare of His people, who are the objects of satanic and Satan-inspired wrath and opposition.

It is only natural to move from this positive aspect of divine vehemence to its messianic implications. In Revelation 5 an elder spoke of Jesus as "the Lion of the tribe of Judah" (v. 5). His leonine qualities may be seen in the later visions of the book. The comparison goes all the way back to Jacob's blessing on Judah in Genesis 49:9.

> You are a lion's cub, O Judah;
>   you return from the prey, my son.
> Like a lion he crouches and lies down,
>   like a lioness—who dares to rouse him?
> The scepter will not depart from Judah,
>   nor the ruler's staff from between his feet,
> until he comes to whom it belongs
>   and the obedience of the nations is his.

According to Revelation 5, Jesus, the Lamb who became the Lion, had earned the right to reveal the details of coming events. By both mercy and judgment He would bring all nations to their knees before Him, thus fulfilling Jacob's prophecy. Because He is the Lion, none will hinder Him from fulfilling all the Father's will. This is the confidence, and the peace, of the saints.

15. Horn

Achilles, the Greek legend goes, was invulnerable to death except in his right heel. To give him immortality, his mother, Thetis, had dipped him by that heel into the River Styx at an early age. But because his heel had not been submerged in the river, he remained vulnerable in that one spot. In the Trojan War, Paris, prince of the defenders, shot an arrow (guided by the god Apollo) that struck Achilles in his right heel, and the hero died. Clearly, the gods of Greece were unable to give complete protection to those who looked to them for help.

In biblical history, a prophet predicted Ahab's death because of his evil deeds. So the king of Israel determined to save himself. Ahab dressed as an ordinary soldier and went into battle, while only Jehoshaphat, king of Judah, wore the garments of royalty. "But someone drew his bow at random and hit the king of Israel between the sections of his armor . . . and that evening he died" (1 Kings 22:34-36). Neither his god Baal nor the military stratagems he devised were able to protect Ahab once God had determined that the time was ripe for judgment.

Among other points, both of these accounts show us how important a *complete* armor is. We cannot count ourselves secure unless we are protected against every kind of attack. For this reason, David—writing "when the Lord delivered him from the hand of all his enemies and from the hand of Saul" (Ps. 18:2)—provided us with a long list of words descriptive of God as his complete helper. David's God was a rock, fortress, deliverer, shield, horn, stronghold, refuge, and savior. The list of images is long because God's protection is so multifaceted and complete.

Calvin's comments are very much to the point:

> David, therefore, by attributing to God various methods of saving his people, protests that, provided he has God for his protector and defender, he is effectually fortified against all peril and assault; as if he had said, Those whom God intends to succour and defend are not only safe against one kind of dangers, but are as it were surrounded by impregnable ramparts on all sides, so that, should a thousand deaths be presented to their view, they ought not to be afraid even at this formidable array.[1]

David called God "the horn of my salvation." The expression probably means little to us living in the twentieth century. But people who lived in David's day feared the horns of wild animals that could gore and kill defenseless people. Horns came to be signs of brute strength and great power. And because Israelites stood in great awe of these beasts, horns also became symbols of great dignity. David was not terrified by God's great power, because he saw that power working for his deliverance from all his enemies, including Saul. Such a view was typical of how saints viewed the divine horn throughout biblical history.

Moses prophesied of Joseph's tribe that

> In majesty he is like a firstborn bull;
>> his horns are like the horns of a wild ox.
> With them he will gore the nations,
>> even those at the ends of the earth
>>>   (Deut. 33:17)

These words were fulfilled when Joshua, a descendant of Joseph, led Israel into the land. "Not one of their enemies withstood them; the Lord handed all their enemies over to them" (Josh. 21:44). The prophecy was further fulfilled under David and Solomon when they led the whole nation in conquering all the kingdoms from the Euphrates to the border of Egypt.

Much later, when Micah was prophesying of Messiah's coming, he foresaw another conquest by Israel, now beleaguered by many surrounding nations:

> Rise and thresh, O Daughter of Zion,
>   for I will give you horns of iron;
> I will give you hoofs of bronze
>   and you will break to pieces many nations.
>   (4:13)

So when David called God his horn, he was thinking of divine omnipotence and swift judgment and the ability to fulfill any promise He had made—no matter how weak His people might seem and how powerful their enemies might appear.

But God was a horn only for the sake of those who believed and obeyed the covenant. Just before the Exile, as Jerusalem was being destroyed, the writer of Lamentations could say in real despair:

> In fierce anger he [God] has cut off
> every horn of Israel. . . .
> he has exalted the horn of your foes.
>   (2:3, 17)

God had reduced the power of Judah to nothing, while the Babylonians did whatever they wanted in the holy city. Such helplessness is the plight of any person or people who forsake the Lord, no matter how bright their past may have been.

This almighty power belonged to Messiah, and He was spoken of as a horn in both Old and New Testaments.

Hannah praised the Lord for lifting high her horn against her foes (a reference to her triumph over the taunts of Peninnah, hitherto the more favored of Elkanah's wives). In her prophetic vision she went well beyond her own situation and saw her victory as part of a cosmic triumph in which God

> will give strength to his king
>   and exalt the horn of his anointed.
>   (1 Sam. 2:10)

Although this could be taken as a prediction of David's might and power, in view of the context it is probably best understood as a reference to Messiah.

In line with this messianic prophecy, Zechariah saw his son, John, as the harbinger of the age spoken of by God to Abraham and David. Note how much Zechariah's words resemble David's in Psalm 18:

> Praise be to the Lord, the God of Israel,
> because he has come and has redeemed his people.
> He has raised up a horn of salvation for us
> in the house of his servant David.
>   (Luke 1:68f.)

Jesus confirmed the application of these words when He bade His disciples good-bye and said, "All authority in heaven and on earth has been given to me. Therefore go...." Clearly, the church has a horn of deliverance, "and the gates of Hades will not overcome it." The apostle John saw Jesus in heaven as a Lamb having seven horns (Rev. 5:6) with universal authority and great wrath. The horns doubtless present a graphic picture of Him as King of Kings and Lord of Lords. Christ will have no problem subduing all the powers of earth and heaven, the Dragon and his followers, "the kings of the earth, the princes, the generals, the rich, the mighty, and every slave and every free man" (6:15). Every saint can say that Jesus is "the horn of my salvation."

Another picture might have come to David's mind when he called God "the horn of my salvation." The altars in both the tabernacle and the temple were provided with horns at the top of each of the four corners. Sometimes sacrifices were tied to these horns (according to one interpretation of Ps. 118:27). At other times blood was smeared on the horns as part of the ritual of atonement, so that the horns came to be reminders of God's power to save. At still other times those in fear of death sought protection by clinging to these horns until their case might be heard (Exod. 21:14; 1 Kings 1:5f.; 2:28ff.).

Hence it was very meaningful for David to include "horn"

among the descriptions of God. The other descriptions of God in our study are largely defensive; only "horn" indicates offensive action. But as our horn the Lord is sufficient for protection from our enemies and for salvation from our sins.

Notes
[1] *Commentary on the Book of Psalms,* 1:261. The rest of Calvin's comments on this verse are well worth reading.

16. Bird

When Israel came out of Egypt, life for the people of God became a very new and different experience. For the first time, they were no longer subject to their Egyptian masters, they were free from heavy labor, and they could make their own decisions.

However, the Israelites were surrounded by hostile forces—environmental and human. Moses called the desert "a barren and howling waste" (Deut. 32:10), far different from homes in "civilized" Egypt. The wandering nation had to be fed day by day amid public health hazards of such proportions as can only boggle the mind. The leaders had to be on the alert against wild beasts of every sort. Furthermore, after they left the Egyptians behind, the Israelites confronted new enemies. Even though they themselves had never been trained to fight, they had to face warlike nations. Clearly they needed protection, direction, and strength.

That Israel succeeded at all was due to the presence of a divine eagle who, as He Himself said, carried the nation on eagles' wings and brought the people to a desert place where He would bless them (Exod. 19:4). During the early months of an eagle's life, its parents' time is consumed wholly in providing food and protection for their young; so had the Lord fed His children and supplied them with water. The eagle spreads its

126

wings to prevent its young from falling when they are ready to leave the nest; so had God kept His own from Egyptian and Amalekite forces.

And even when God's people were faithless and had grumbled because of the newness of their situation, He had put up with them and overlooked their shortcomings. The young eagles had much to learn; becoming mature would take much exercise on their part and much more patience on the part of their divine parent. All this loving attention was in contrast to the judgment He had brought on the Egyptians: "You yourselves have seen what I did to Egypt."

Later on, Moses described these events, elaborating on the figure:

> In a desert land he found him,
>   in a barren and howling waste,
> He shielded him and cared for him;
>   he guarded him as the apple of his eye.
> (Deut. 32:10)

Moses placed emphasis both on what might have happened but did not and on what, in fact, did occur. God's protection kept Israel from many a pitfall: no insuperable problem was met with during those days of desert wandering. When they might have met with enemies that could have frightened them, He led the Israelites by another way (Exod. 13:17f.). When they did err, it was because they chose to; they were not overwhelmed by circumstances over which there was no control.

God's protecting care was not confined to the Exodus and conquest of Canaan. As we saw in the chapter on wild beasts, God as lion protected Judah from Sennacherib. In a quick shift of figures, Isaiah predicted that same action by God as of a bird protecting a nest:

> Like birds hovering overhead,
>   the Lord Almighty will shield Jerusalem;
> he will shield it and deliver it,
>   he will "pass over" it and will rescue it.
> (31:5)

The translators of the *New International Version* have evidently placed the words *pass over* in quotation marks to highlight the fact that these same words are used in Exodus for the Passover event, and they are used nowhere else. Just as the destroying angel had passed *through* Egypt but *over* the Israelites, so he would pass *through* the Assyrians but *over* Jerusalem (cf. Isa. 37:36). After hundreds of years, the Eagle was still hovering over His people.

Psalms 17 and 57

But there were also dangers and enemies within the nation itself. As we have seen in other chapters, protection was much on David's mind as he fled from King Saul and later from his own son, Absalom; and in the psalms ascribed to him, sheltering wings are a frequent figure of speech. In Psalm 17 David may well have had Deuteronomy 32 in mind (see above) when he called upon God:

> Keep me as the apple of your eye;
>   hide me in the shadow of your wings.
>
> (Ps. 17:8)

Wicked people were surrounding and assailing him (v. 9). M'Caw and Motyer, commenting on the Psalms in the *New Bible Commentary: Revised*, suggest that this verse may refer to David's experiences in Maon (cf. 1 Sam. 23:26) where Saul was pursuing him.[1] A Philistine raid diverted Saul's attention, and so David was delivered. He called the name of the place Sela Hammahlekoth, which means "rock or parting," for there Saul left off following him. Once again, the divine eagle had brought protection.

In a psalm identified as having been written when David fled from Saul into a cave, we have a prayer probably uttered soon after that experience at Maon. David called on God for mercy, stating that he would take refuge in the shadow of His wings until the disaster had passed (57:1). How God delivered him is a familiar story (1 Sam. 24:1ff.). David describes his peril in two ways. He was surrounded by lions and other ravenous beasts (Ps. 57:4); then, evil people spread a net and dug a pit for him (v. 6). In both cases he felt overpowered and perhaps outwitted. Only God could deliver him, and God did just that. David will live to give God the credit among the nations so that His glory will be over all the earth (v. 11).

In both Psalms 17 and 57 David's protection came in answer to prayer. He was aware of his danger and prayed about it. In the Lord's Prayer one of the petitions is "deliver us from the evil one." By this we are advised that evil is constantly surrounding the Christian, and prayer for protection from it is always appropriate. And it is just as appropriate to expect the deliverance that comes from the shadow of God's wings.

Psalms 36, 63, and 91

In Psalm 36 David described another deliverance from the sinfulness of the wicked. The experience, whatever it was, made a profound impression on him:

> How priceless is your unfailing love!
> Both high and low among men
> find refuge in the shadow of your wings.
>
> (v. 7)

God's love, faithfulness, righteousness, and justice had combined to protect David from wicked people. On the one hand, it was as natural for God to do this for His saint as for a hen to spread her wings to protect her chicks. But on the other hand, for the great God of heaven to do this for mere creatures—this was priceless indeed! We should never let the wonder of deliverance become a commonplace experience.

Psalm 63 may have been written during those days when David and his men were refugees in the desert of Judah. They enjoyed God's protection throughout those days, and at the end of each day they could ponder the regularity of God's help:

On my bed I remember you;
  I think of you through the watches of the night.
Because you are my help,
  I will sing in the shadow of your wings.
                                        (vv. 6, 7)

In the desert David could not visit the sanctuary as he had in times past. He had seen God's power and glory portrayed in the furniture of the tabernacle and in the sacrifices performed there (v. 2). Now, miles away, he nevertheless experienced that power and glory as God provided for him and his men in the wilderness. David promised to sing God's praises for that protection. In the reference to the Lord's wings, some have seen an allusion to the wings of the cherubim that overshadowed the mercy seat in the Holy of Holies. If that interpretation is accepted, then David was promising to return to the tabernacle at some future date, and there he would celebrate the kindness of the Lord who had protected him so wonderfully. Since God was his protector, David knew he would survive to return to normal activities.

Psalm 91 brings together two names of the Lord: "Most High" and "Almighty" *(Shaddai)*. God will provide shelter and shadow, will be a refuge and a fortress, for those who trust in Him.

The promises of protection from harm that follow seem so absolute and all-inclusive that we may be led to think that a Christian would never, under any circumstances, endure hardship or calamity. However, the psalmist was not making such a blanket prediction. He was promising that we will be delivered from snares of Satan and of evil people and from the punishment of the wicked. When such awful things occur, we may trust in the feathers and wings of divine favor. But equally, just as chicks need to be nudged from the nest to learn how to be mature and productive in this world, so Christians may expect the testing, the chastening, and the suffering that produce godly virtues (Rom. 5:3f.).

The eagle does far more for its nestlings than give them protection. The parent eagle must train its young for life as adult birds. So God was now prepared to give the Israelites a way of life that would make other nations envy their wisdom and understanding (cf. Deut. 4:5ff.). Moses called this training a "stirring up" (32:10). As the eagle knows just when the eaglets are ready to fly, so God planned experiences for the people that were adapted to their abilities.

The Church Age

Twice, as Paul recalled these desert experiences in 1 Corinthians 10:6 and 11, he reminded his readers that "these things occurred as examples [or types]." Not only were the failures of the Israelites to be understood as warnings, but God's acts were to be interpreted as normative for all time. God's providence is directed to teaching His people lessons preparing them for this life and the life to come. As the faithful parent eagle, He trains us in holiness by the day-to-day experiences He brings into our lives.

But the stirring up of the nest has still another side. God in His providence stirs His people up so that they will accomplish His will. Israel by itself would never have left Egypt and entered Canaan. That the people did so was because God would not let them alone. He kept after them until His purpose was done. Similarly, in the New Testament we see the divine eagle stirring up the nest. In Acts 8 a great persecution came upon the church. Paul certainly had a hand in this; he went "from house to house" dragging off men and women to put them in prison. He was very efficient in his work so that "all except the apostles" fled and were scattered throughout Judea and Samaria (Acts 8:1). This persecution was a terrifying experience for the young Christians, but they would not have fulfilled God's command (Acts 1:8) unless something had upset their lives to cause them to move.

So the troubled people fled, and they "preached the word wherever they went." Jesus' prediction that Samaria would soon be reaped (John 4:35) was fulfilled as the result of this persecution.

When troubles beset the church, they may be due to satanic opposition. But they also may be the result of the Eagle's stirring up. This is true also of individuals. Paul may have felt that his imprisonment was Satan's work; it was also the work of the Spirit, and people were saved as a result. "I want you to know, brothers, that what has happened to me has really served to advance the gospel" (Phil. 1:12).

What the eagle does by instinct is not an act of cruelty, even though the eaglets probably do not appreciate it. Similarly, God's providences, though sometimes painful, are acts of love. But such insight is not easy to come by. Moses lamented, "If only they were wise and would understand this and discern what their end will be!" (Deut. 32:29).

Ruth

When Ruth vowed to stay with Naomi so that "your God [will be] my God," great changes came into her life. On the human level, Ruth gained an inheritance and a new husband as well as a place in the genealogy of the Messiah; in God's sight the young woman placed herself under the wings of the God of Israel where she would always find refuge (Ruth 2:12).

It was Boaz, not Naomi, who had this insight. Naomi had little regard for God's covenant and its blessings. If Ruth had followed her mother-in-law's advice (1:8-13), she would have had none of these benefits. (We should not be too hard on Naomi. She had met with many sorrows and had not lived with the covenant people for years, with the result that her spirit had become bitter [1:20f.]. Nonetheless Naomi was quite wrong in her advice.) But God's electing grace overcame human short-sightedness and earthbound wisdom.

Boaz saw Ruth not only as a potential bride but as a trophy of grace, now partaking of the blessings of Abraham and his children. In many ways, Ruth exemplifies the believer—once an alien and now a member of the family of God, but always fragile, often in peril, ever needing a defender.

Earlier in this chapter we saw God as the bird flying in the heavens to bring protection and direction to His people. In the Book of Ruth, the figure is of a bird on the ground offering protection to her chicks from whatever perils they might face in the barnyard. In many ways the metaphor of a parent bird illustrates both God's concern for His own and His power to protect them from all kinds of evil.

First, God protected the young widow as she gleaned in the fields of Boaz (Ruth 2:9, 22). Then He moved in the heart of her nearest kinsman so that he was willing to relinquish his rights to Elimelech's estate and, thus, give Boaz the freedom to marry her. Finally, He opened her womb so that she would have a son, Obed, who was of the line of the coming Messiah. And all of this happened to one who had originally worshiped Chemosh, the god of the Moabites.

In His lament over Jerusalem, Jesus showed how people in His generation differed from Ruth. She gave up her worship of idols, embraced the covenant, and enjoyed its blessings to the full. Though instructed in all the law and the prophets, the Jews were nevertheless unwilling to recognize the Lord of the covenant and His grace, and so their house is left to them desolate (Matt. 23:38). But that was their preference. He had offered them what He had given Ruth. "How often I have longed to gather your children together, as a hen gathers her chicks under her wings, but you were not willing!" (Luke 13:34).

We should not confine God's gracious offer to the time of Jesus' ministry. Clearly, the words of the prophets were an important part of this invitation. But the Jews had killed the prophets and stoned those who had been sent to them. When people reject God's gracious offer of salvation, they choose instead the desolation of divine rejection and judgment.

Notes
[1] P. 460.

Part Four

Occupations
as
Mirrors of His Glory

17. Warrior

The children of Israel had been slaves—brickmakers and brick-layers—for many generations in Egypt. They were unskilled in war; they had never studied any military strategy. Yet Pharaoh and his army, with all his experience and prowess, could not conquer God's people. During the plagues, the Hebrews had been irrepressible. And later on in the Exodus itself, they could not be destroyed, even though the Egyptians showed great skill by trapping them by the sea.

It was Israel's God who had made the difference. Miriam and Moses made this fact plain when they sang the song of deliverance recorded in Exodus 15. Israel triumphed because God had been the strategist and the unrelenting warrior:

> *Your* right hand, O Lord,
>   was majestic in power.
> *Your* right hand, O Lord,
>   shattered the enemy.
>
> (v. 6, emphasis added)

From the very beginning, God's people were to know that they were different. They were aliens in a strange land, often at odds with their neighbors. Abraham would not accept the booty from the king of Sodom (Gen. 14:22). Isaac was not to marry a daughter of the Canaanites (24:3). Israel as a nation was to evict those who were living in Canaan, making neither covenant nor armed truce with them (Exod. 23:31f.).

So during the times in its history when Israel was truly faithful, tension and, often, open warfare continued with neighboring tribes and peoples. But the opposition was never merely political. As one nation among others, Israel had no inherent right to oppose its neighbors and take their possessions. The rights of God's people came from the sovereign Lord, and their opposition was God-given. Because He had chosen them, they were to be freed from Egypt; because He had chosen the land for them, they could invade it. Neither the Exodus nor the conquest of the Promised Land was accomplished by their own prowess. The Jews prospered in battle because "the Lord is a warrior."

Israel had enemies because the Lord had enemies. Sin was both the occasion and the cause for the Lord's enmity, and so there was enmity between God and the Amorites. But in Abraham's day "the sin of the Amorites had not yet reached its full measure" (Gen. 15:16). Four hundred years later, when sin had ripened for judgment, Joshua and the people were God's instrument in the war against God's enemies.

All this was made clear to Joshua as he contemplated his role as leader of the armies of Israel. Although he had been leader for some years (Exod. 17:8ff.), fighting in Canaan was a new experience. As the time to conquer Jericho drew near, Joshua was suddenly confronted by a warlike figure, "a man standing in front of him with a drawn sword in his hand" (Josh. 5:13). Joshua posed a perfectly natural question, asking in effect, "Are you on our side or theirs?" But a question in that form could not truly be answered by either a yes or a no. The question betrayed a partisanship based on worldly considerations rather than on a covenantal understanding of God and His rule in the world. So the stranger answered, "Neither . . . but as commander of the army of the Lord I have now come."

The question Joshua should have asked was "Are *we* on the Lord's side?"—for that is where the emphasis should have been.

There is a critical difference between the Lord's being on our side and our being on His side. In the former we often try to make God a partner to our partisan ways and ask Him to do what we want Him to do (for example, when we pray that God give us success). In the latter we ally ourselves with God and His kingdom and seek the fulfillment of His purposes.

The "man" who appeared to Joshua was obviously a theophany (an appearance of God). He had come not only to stress that Joshua should rearrange his priorities but also to encourage him specifically, that as He had been with Moses so now He would be with Joshua (1:5).

The command from the "man" that Joshua remove his sandals because the ground was holy would certainly remind Joshua of God's earlier appearance to Moses at the burning bush. As God had commanded Israel in the battle with Pharaoh, so now He would lead Joshua and the people against the cities of Canaan.

The later history of Israel is replete with examples of God's fighting for His people and against their enemies. The Lord, as the supreme strategist, used many tactics in His war against evil. Sometimes He won victories without Israel's help, sometimes He used them as instruments of His power. Though God's tactics changed, several principles remained the same.

First, God's people must be holy when they go into battle. This entailed obedience to His commands. When they disobeyed, He was not with them in battle (Josh. 7). Holiness also involved having a confidence in Him, not a divided loyalty or allegiance to another nation (Isa. 31:1-3). This meant the people of God had to be willing to stand alone and not become allied with other nations (2 Chron. 19:2).

Attitude also played an important role in Israel's battles. After Jehoshaphat had been healed by God, his "heart was proud and he did not respond to the kindness shown him: therefore the Lord's wrath was on him and on Judah and Jerusalem" (2 Chron. 33:25). In such a state of mind the king was in no condition to lead the nation into battle.

In addition, God's people had to live by faith. But faith is expressed in several ways. It may be a waiting, passive faith that watched God do it all: "You will not have to fight this battle. Take up your positions; stand firm and see the deliverance the Lord will give you" (2 Chron. 20:17). Or it might be a dynamic, active faith that fought as though the outcome depended entirely upon the warriors (2 Chron. 14:11-15).

The main point in all of this for us is to rely on God's wisdom and never to conduct ourselves as though God works only in one way. Just as Satan has his schemes of warfare (2 Cor. 2:11; Eph. 6:11), so God has His strategic plan for all of history. God's people must not only be on His side in the battle, they must also have insight to know their place in His plan. The overall blueprint is found in the Scriptures; the details unfold each day in His providence.

Jeremiah 21:5

It was a sad day in Israel when the people discovered that the Lord had switched sides and was now the commander of heathen forces arrayed against them and His temple and holy city. Here again the biblical imagery becomes disturbing and unsettling. The northern kingdom had turned against the Lord and had given themselves to idolatry, and Judah was not far behind. Isaiah could say,

> They have harps and lyres at their banquets,
>   tambourines and flutes and wine,
> but they have no regard for the deeds of the Lord,
>   no respect for the work of his hands.
>
> (5:12)

God's people were no longer concerned with being on His side.

His response to their apostasy was to lead other nations against Israelitish cities. In the Book of Lamentations, the author looked on with horror as the Babylonians sacked the holy city. His horror was compounded because he saw not only the Babylonians at work but the Lord, the covenant God of Israel, as well.

The Lord has rejected
   all the warriors in my midst;
he has summoned an army against me
   to crush my young men.
In his winepress the Lord has trampled
   the Virgin Daughter of Judah.
                                (1:15)

In reading chapter 2 of the same book, one is impressed by the fact that the Babylonians were never mentioned as the destroyers of dwellings, strongholds, palaces, temple, altar, walls, and gates. The author ascribed all the destruction to the Lord: "The Lord is like an enemy. . . . The Lord has done what he planned; he has fulfilled his word, which he decreed long ago" (vv. 5, 17).

Israel had forgotten God's message to Joshua. Instead, the people trusted that God would be on their side just because they had been the holy nation and Jerusalem had been the holy city. To encourage themselves in this they would stand outside the temple and chant,

> This is the temple of the Lord, the temple of the Lord, the temple of the Lord. (Jer. 7:4)

But these were deceptive words. Judah had now joined the nations of the world in worshiping other gods and trusting in alliances with other countries, and the temple of the Lord had become a den of robbers (cf. Jer. 7:11; Mark 11:17).

So God directed nation after nation against His people. Finally the Assyrians destroyed Israel, and the Babylonians sacked Jerusalem. Only righteousness exalts a nation, but sin is a disgrace to any people (Prov. 14:34).

Isaiah 13:4

Following his indictment of Israel and Judah and predictions that the Lord would turn against both of them, Isaiah turned to the nations of the world and spoke of their lot as enemies of the living God. First, Babylon, after a period of time in ascendancy, was to be attacked by the Medes (13:17). Then judgment was pronounced against Assyria, the Philistines, Moab, Syria, Cush, Egypt, Edom, and Tyre (chaps. 13-23). Isaiah summed it all up with these words:

> See, the Lord is coming out of his dwelling
> to punish the people of the earth for their sins.
> (26:21)

Although He used many of these pagan nations to chastise and punish His own people, the Lord provoked the Gentiles against each other so that their supremacy was usually short-lived. We have here a view of the history of the nations as God directs their risings and fallings. He has a purpose in history— to honor His name and to redeem His people. And He has a standard of conduct He enforces on all nations by which they stand or fall, prosper or lack. We should listen to our newscasts and read our newspapers with this fact in mind. As the events of history unfold before our eyes, God works as a Man of War, conducting His battle with nations and bringing them to account.

Ephesians 6:12

In the New Testament the church has become the holy nation (cf. Exod. 19:5f.; 1 Pet. 2:9f.). The focus on the enemy has shifted from God's war against nations to His battle against demonic powers. But in saying this we should make two qualifications. First, even in the Old Testament, demons had been seen as influencing the affairs of nations (Dan. 10). So, the shift is one of degree, not of kind. Second, God continues His control over the nations and uses their armies for His purposes (Luke 21:20ff.).

Still, there is room for the generalization that as God destroyed cities given over to idolatry, so now He destroys "strongholds . . . arguments and every pretension that sets itself up against the knowledge of God" (2 Cor. 10:4f.). A great war is being waged for and against the kingdom of God, and, as we said above, the daily news should be read in the light of this truth. Moreover, the principles that governed the people of God in the Old Testament should once again guide the saints in their obedience to God as a Man of War (cf. the preceding comments on Isa. 13:4).

The idea of warfare might seem unsettling to people who remember Jesus' words, "Blessed are the peacemakers" (Matt. 5:9). Yet we must remember that truth has many sides. We are called to be peacemakers, but we are also warned that "while people are saying, 'Peace and safety,' destruction will come on them suddenly" (1 Thess. 5:3). Moreover, Jesus said:

> Do not suppose that I have come to bring peace to the earth. I did not come to bring peace, but a sword. For I have come to turn
> "a man against his father,
>   a daughter against her mother,
> a daughter-in-law against her mother-in-law—
>   a man's enemies will be the members of his own household."
>   (Matt. 10:35f.)

In keeping with our remarks that figures of speech can unsettle and nudge us out of our complacency, we may quote Herman Ridderbos,

> This tremendous dynamic of the divine coming which sets the world of angels in motion (Matt. 1; Luke 2); fills the devil's empire with alarm (Matt. 4:3ff.; Mark 1:24; Matt. 12:29); yes, even causes Satan to fall from heaven (Luke 10:18), permeates and transmits itself in everything and in all who are touched by it. For the coming of the kingdom is the initial stage of the great drama of the history of the end. It throws man and the world into a crisis. . . . It confronts man with the necessity of making all-important decisions that will rule his whole existence. Its coming should rouse everybody from their false rest and complacency.[1]

In truth, God is waging war against Satan, leading up to the latter's final judgment and destruction. Similarly, Satan is waging war against the Lord and His Christ, struggling to thwart God's purposes.

Paul was aware of satanic opposition to his evangelistic travels (1 Thess. 2:18), and he called the Ephesians to struggle against demonic powers and schemes (6:11). He called Timothy "to endure hardship with us like a good soldier of Christ Jesus" (2 Tim. 2:3). The apostle himself could claim "I have fought the good fight" (4:7). As William Hendriksen wrote,

> It had been a fight against Satan; against the principalities and powers, the world-rulers of this darkness in the heavenlies; against Jewish and pagan vice and violence; against Judaism among the Galatians; against fanaticism among the Thessalonians; against contention, fornication and litigation among the Corinthians; against incipient Gnosticism among the Ephesians and Colossians; against fightings without and fears within; and last but not least, against the law of sin and death operating within his own heart.[2]

Paul could with confidence wage such a battle all his Christian life and urge others to do the same because he was persuaded that Jesus had "disarmed the powers and authorities, . . . made a public spectacle of them, triumphing over them by the cross" (Col. 2:15).

Although the battle has been won and the final outcome is certain, the struggle goes on. Paul could write to the Philippians,

> For it has been granted to you on behalf of Christ not only to believe on him, but also to suffer for him. (1:29)

In view of this struggle, the apostle urged the Christians in Philippi to stand firm and contend for the faith (1:27).

The apostle John most vividly portrays the cosmic battle. It is waged in heaven between Michael and his angels against the Dragon and his angels (Rev. 12:7). It is waged on earth as the Dragon, enraged against the saints, goes to war against the woman and her offspring. The battle culminates in the coming of Christ riding upon a white horse. He strikes down the nations, rules with an iron scepter, and treads the winepress of the fury of the wrath of God (Rev. 19:14ff.).

Though, in our time, the focus may have changed, one thing has not changed. God still is the commander of His army. The question is not, Is He on our side? but rather, Are we on His side?

His promise to be with His people came after His command that they disciple the nations (Matt. 28:20). Too often we ignore the command and still want God to fulfill the promise. That is why we need to pay attention to the Lord's message to Joshua.

Notes
[1] *The Coming of the Kingdom*, 27.
[2] *Exposition of the Pastoral Epistles*, 315.

18. Bookkeeper

Years ago, my mother asked me to go to the cleaners to pick up a suit belonging to my father. Arriving there, I told the cleaner what I wanted and then waited while he went looking for the suit. I noticed a framed certificate on one of the walls of the room in which the picture of an eye was in a prominent place. An inscription read something like, "The all-seeing eye of God is upon you." I took only a few seconds to read those words and then ran home home as quickly as I could—without the suit. I told my mother I would never go back to that place again. "God is there, and I don't want Him looking at me!"

I suspect my experience was not all that atypical. Who likes to be reminded that God knows and remembers all the things we do? I recall a middle-aged skeptic confronted with the thought that God will judge us for what we have done. He scoffed at the idea and asked, "Do you mean to tell me that God has nothing better to do than watch me every minute of the day and mark down everything I do?" Here he walked across the floor, toeing an imaginary line, sneering as he went.[1]

No, the idea of God as a bookkeeper will not be a popular doctrine today.[2] On the human level we resent the fact that data about us, things we like to consider our own affairs and "none of your business," are collected and stored. We like our privacy.

And when someone else knows too much about us, we feel that our liberties have been abridged.

Beyond what we conceive to be a loss of privacy and freedom, we don't like to be held accountable to others. Because we live in a modern, complex society in which these invasions of privacy seem to be necessary, we grudgingly accept them but protest against them whenever the opportunity presents itself.

Scriptures make plain that God's omniscience covers every aspect of our lives. The psalmist confessed that his life had been written in advance:

> All the days ordained for me
> were written in your book
> before one of them came to be.
>
> (Ps. 139:16)

Here the word "ordained" literally is "formed," a word we shall meet again when we look at God as a potter. The word appears several times in the Genesis account of creation. The sense goes beyond a decree or decision, and it indicates that God takes an active part in shaping the days of our lives. Having thus formed our lives, God holds before Him as in a book our day-by-day experiences. There is no place for chance, luck, or fortune. What a comfort this is when life seems so confused!

It is also a comfort to know that God remembers our good deeds. Nehemiah was jealous not for his reputation in human history but for his place in God's favor. He had worked hard for his people, and he called on God to remember his labors (5:19; 13:22, 31). He did not present his deeds as the ground of his acceptance before God (in fact, he spoke of mercy and covenant-love), but neither did he consider his works of no consequence. In 13:14 he used the language of bookkeeping when he asked God, "do not blot out what I have faithfully done."

Malachi stressed the same truth. In his days there were many skeptics regarding God's righteousness and love. The faithful needed reassurance, and so they banded together for mutual encouragement. God heard their conversation and caused a book of remembrance to be written about them and their fidelity to His cause:

"They will be mine," says the Lord Almighty, "in the day when I make up my treasured possession." (3:17)

This remembrance on God's part is a matter of grace, but it is also a matter of justice. The Hebrew Christians also had suffered much because of their confession that Jesus is the Messiah. Though they were deeply troubled then, they were also greatly assured that a rich reward lay ahead for them, guaranteed by the fairness of God: "God is not unjust; he will not forget your work and the love you have shown him as you have helped his people and continue to help them" (Heb. 6:10).

The point to all this is that whereas good works have no place in our justification, they have a necessary place in our sanctification (cf. 1 Tim. 6:18; 2 Tim. 3:17; Titus 2:7; 3:8, 14). In our zeal for grace over works, we should not forget that grace produces good works in the lives of Christians. At the time of the Reformation many disdained works even for Christians because they seemed to obscure the grace of God; the greater the sin, the greater the exhibition of grace! The Reformation doctrine of sanctification was developed in response to this. One expression of that doctrine is found in chapter 16 of the *Westminster Confession of Faith*. [3]

Another great comfort to Christians is that their prayers are recorded and remembered. David writes of this in Psalm 56:8:

Record my lament;
  list my tears on your scroll—
are they not in your record?

If we follow the cue of the superscription, David uttered this prayer when the Philistines had seized him in Gath (1 Sam. 21:10ff.). He had gone among them because Saul was pursuing him and so there was no place for him in Israel. It was going to be a long, drawn-out struggle, and David would have to be on the run from both his own countrymen and their enemies. He asked God to remember his prayer during this period as a fugitive.

It is true that not all prayers are answered immediately or

even shortly. This is why they must be recorded. David may have waited ten years until his prayer for deliverance was fully answered and the royal throne was his. In the nineteenth century, George Muller prayed for the salvation of two men for twenty-five years before they were converted.

Our prayers stand recorded in the scroll of God, and this we must remember when tempted to say that God has forgotten. To resist that suggestion, the Christian will pray, "Are they not in Your record?"

By far the greatest number of passages about God as bookkeeper relate to the record of our sins and their removal through forgiveness. God warned Isaiah concerning Israel:

> See, it stands written before me:
>> I will not keep silent but will pay back in full:
>> I will pay it back into their laps—
> both your sins and the sins of your fathers.
>> (65:6, 7)

Such a thought has had a profound influence in the lives of many of God's leaders.

As a young boy, Martin Luther went with his family to a church where he saw in a stained-glass window the figure of Christ coming in judgment, a parchment scroll in his hands. Sometimes he sang the hymn "Dies Irae," a song remembered today only in crossword puzzles. Although many will dismiss the hymn as morbid and even heretical, it expresses a profound biblical truth:

> Day of wrath! O day of mourning!
>> See fulfilled the prophets' warning,
>> Heav'n and earth in ashes burning! . . .
> Lo! the book, exactly worded,
>> Wherein all hath been recorded:
>> Thence shall judgment be awarded.

When he had come to manhood and entered the priesthood, Luther remembered the window and hymn and their message. He came under conviction for sin and became terrified by the thought of what was written in God's book about him. He sought to ease his guilt and fears by engaging in a variety of ceremonies and works, until he realized that what had been recorded, frightening as it was, could be removed from the book by the same God who wrote it. Luther found his hope in the epistles to the Romans and Galatians, though he was also lecturing on the Psalms in those days and might have found the truth there.

Consider Psalm 32:

> Blessed is he
>> whose transgressions are forgiven,
>> whose sins are covered.
> Blessed is the man
>> whose sin the Lord does not count against him
>> and in whose spirit is no deceit.
>> (vv. 1, 2; Rom. 4:7-8)

The English Puritan John Owen, greatly influenced by Psalm 130, wrote a commentary on it of more than three hundred pages. Twenty pages are devoted to verse 3:

> If you, O Lord, kept a record of sins,
>> O Lord who could stand?

What an overpowering thought the omniscience of God is. If He has recorded all I have thought, said, and done, what hope is there for me when I stand in judgment? Owen devoted most of his book (227 pages) to verse 4:

> But with you there is forgiveness;
>> therefore you are feared.

When God forgives the sins of those who put their trust in Him, the record of sins is thereby removed. This is what we mean when we say that God will remember our sins no more (Jer. 31:34). It does not mean that they are erased from His omniscience (for then He would cease to be God), but they are no longer held against the believer. Jesus the Messiah died for us that God might "demonstrate his justice at the present time, so as to be just and the one who justifies the man who has faith in Jesus" (Rom. 3:26).

Another line of truth has to do with a book bearing the names of those who outwardly profess faith in God. Moses knew of the existence of such a volume, and he was willing to have his name erased from it for the sake of Israel, who had just sinned by worshiping the calf (Exod. 32:33f.). God refused to do this but replied, "Whoever has sinned against me I will blot out of my book." No doubt this was a reference to those who had followed Moses out of Egypt but had so easily succumbed to idolatry at the first temptation. As Paul later described them, they

> were all under the cloud and . . . they all passed through the sea. They were all baptized into Moses in the cloud and in the sea. They all ate the same spiritual food and drank the same spiritual drink; for they drank from the spiritual rock that accompanied them, and that rock was Christ. Nevertheless, God was not pleased with most of them; their bodies were scattered over the desert. (1 Cor. 10:1-5)

In one of the harshest of imprecatory psalms, David prayed concerning his enemies:

> Charge them with crime upon crime;
>   do not let them share in your salvation.
> May they be blotted out of the book of life
>   and not be listed with the righteous.
>   (Ps. 69:27f.)

This psalm is one of the most quoted passages in the New Testament (cf. John 15:25; 2:17; Rom. 15:3; Matt. 27:34, 48 and parallels; Rom. 11:9-10; Rev. 16:1; Acts 1:20; Phil. 4:3; Rev. 3:5; 13:8; 17:8; 20:12, 15; 21:27). The psalm may have been written during or just after Absalom's rebellion, and the evil man spoken of may well have been Ahithophel. Many see in him a type of Judas—the familiar friend turned traitor who took his own life when he realized that he had failed.

And yet Jesus promised the overcomers in Sardis, "I will

never erase his name from the book of life, but will acknowledge his name before my Father and his angels" (Rev. 3:5).

F. F. Bruce may well be correct in his interpretation of these verses:

> The "book of life" appears here . . . to include at first all those whose names are on the membership roll of a local church on earth, but those whose membership is but nominal have their names deleted—i.e., the Lord declares that He never knew them.[4]

This is a warning to those who take their Christianity lightly and have no deep and abiding faith. They seem to share in the blessings of the covenant but, like the Israelites of old, with many of them God is displeased.

The Bible also speaks of the Book of Life in passages that encourage the truly faithful when they are persecuted and become weary. This book belongs to the Lamb of God (Rev. 13:8; 21:27) and was written before creation (17:8). It contains the names of those who will be admitted to heaven (21:27). Those whose names are not written there worship the evil beasts pictured in the Apocalypse (13:8; 17:8).

An angel told Daniel about a time of great distress in which His people would be delivered (12:1). "His people" are defined not ethnically but by the words "everyone whose name is found written in the book." By means of this "book," which promises blessings to those whose names are therein and judgment to those not included, God stresses the vast gulf between the saved and the lost. He emphasizes as well that it is the Lamb of God who makes the difference. As Peter put it, "Salvation is found in no one else, for there is no other name under heaven given to men by which we must be saved" (Acts 4:12).

Notes
[1] I am happy to report that in later years he did confess his faith in God.
[2] I am indebted to Mitchell Dahood for suggesting this figure of speech (cf. *The Anchor Bible: Psalms*).
[3] Sec. 5. "We cannot by our best works merit pardon of sin, or eternal life

at the hand of God, by reason of the great disproportion that is between them and the glory to come; and the infinite distance that is between us and God, whom, by them, we can neither profit, nor satisfy for the debt of our former sins, but when we have done all we can, we have done but our duty, and are unprofitable servants: and because, as they are good, they proceed from His Spirit; and as they are wrought by us, they are defiled, and mixed with so much weakness and imperfection, that they cannot endure the severity of God's judgment."

Sec. 6. "Notwithstanding, the persons of believers being accepted through Christ, their good works are also accepted in Him; not as though they were in this life wholly unblameable and unreprovable in God's sight; but that He, looking upon them in His Son, is pleased to accept and reward that which is sincere, although accompanied with many weaknesses and imperfections."

[4] *The International Bible Commentary*, 1603. For a similar thought without the figure of speech, cf. Matt. 10:33; Luke 12:8; 13:25ff.

19. Judge/Lawyer

I once heard a preacher say that he received no comfort from the thought that God is righteous. The very doctrine made him afraid. He was comforted, he said, only by the teaching that God is love.

I also heard of an old saint on her deathbed who was asked why she could approach death with such peace and calm. Her response was, "The righteousness of God." When pressed as to why that particular doctrine gave her comfort, she replied, "Because a righteous God cannot condemn me once I have been justified in Jesus. He won't hold me accountable when my debt has been paid."

There is, of course, a truth in both statements. There is both a warning and a comfort in the knowledge that God is righteous and holy, but the dying woman was closer to the full truth, as we shall see.

Under the pictures of judge and lawyer, God reveals once again His righteousness and holiness.[1] While He sometimes inveighs against false gods and demons, against wicked nations and individuals, He also prosecutes and passes judgment on His own people for their misdeeds. But also the Lord, as attorney and judge, defends His people from the lies of wicked people and demons.

God's Case Against the Gods

The Israelites had plenty of evidence in their own history of the power of the Lord against idols. It was clearly to be seen in the plagues of Egypt when God showed the impotence of Egyptian deities—the Nile ran red, the sun was darkened, cattle were struck with disease, Pharaoh's son was struck dead. Though not as explicit, the conquest of the Promised Land was also a duel between Israel's God and the many Baals of Canaan. Rahab reported to the spies how the people of Jericho reacted when they heard of the Exodus and of the battles on the other side of Jordan (Josh. 2:8ff.).

But Israel soon forgot the Lord and His mighty acts and became enamored of other gods who, in their minds, were superior to Him. When God began to fulfill the threats of the covenant and Israel began to grow weaker in relation to surrounding nations, it did seem plausible that God had lost His power. Sennacherib's field commander stressed this in his speech to Hezekiah's counselors and to the people nearby (Isa. 36:4ff.). Clearly it was time for the divine attorney to plead His own case.

The case is set forth in moving passages in Isaiah 40-48, where God presents his threefold charge against false gods, especially the gods of the Babylonians.[2] In 41:21 and following, the Lord said, "Present your case . . . so that we may know that you are gods." The Hebrew word translated "case" has a range of applications. Andersen and Freedman describe them as follows:

> The verb . . . never describes an appeal or a call to repentance, but always a hostile confrontation, an accusation. It refers to an angry quarrel or altercation, in any situation, with more formal application to disputation in a court of law.[3]

It is clear that this was not a round-table discussion among friends. The Lord was angry that false gods were being worshiped and angry at their worshipers. In verse 24 He said to the idols, "He who chooses you is detestable." But the "case" the idols were commanded to present was never made. Idols are deaf and dumb; they do not hear the challenge and cannot speak. But the Lord made His argument with zeal and effectiveness.

The case, stated over and over again, showed how useless the idols really were.

1. Idols are *made* by carpenters and blacksmiths, but the Lord *made* the heavens and the earth (see esp. 44:9-20).

God's case against the idols is dripping with irony. Look at the blacksmith who makes an idol out of a bar of metal. He needs to be very strong for the task, but he is worn out as he pounds the metal into shape. It must take a lot of power and a long time to make a god (v. 12)! The carpenter needs not so much brute strength but care and skill as he measures with a tape, marks the wood with a compass, and outlines the god's shape on the plank of wood. He takes a human being as his model and works hard so that the finished product will be thought good enough to be housed in a shrine (vv. 13-14).

But prior to the carpenter's work is the labor of the lumberman. He must wait until the trees—cedars, cypress, oak, or pine—are ready to be gods. It must take a long time to grow a god! Then, and not until then, does he cut the tree down. But wait! An entire tree is too big for a god, so the woodsman chooses only part for the carpenter. Other parts will be used as fuel to bake bread or roast meat or perchance to heat the house.

The idol to which many will bow down is really no different from firewood. The lumberman has chosen *this* pile to be fuel, *that* pile to be god. Suppose he had chosen the other way around? Then people would worship *this* pile and warm themselves with *that* pile. Idols are not only made by mere humans, but mere humans chose which materials will be worshiped!

We should not pay attention to the pieces of wood and stone we call idols. It is the people who are to be charged with stupidity:

> No one stops to think,
>   no one has the knowledge or the understanding to say,
> "Half of it I used for fuel;
>   I even baked bread over its coals,
>   I roasted meat and I ate.
> Shall I make a detestable thing from what is left?
>   Shall I bow down to a block of wood?"

He feeds on ashes, a deluded heart misleads him;
>   he cannot save himself, or say,
> "Is not this thing in my right hand a lie?"
>> (vv. 19-20)

By contrast God *made* Israel. This refers not to the act of physical creation but to the spiritual birth of the people at the time of the Exodus. God Himself draws the consequences of this redemptive act: the Israelites are His servants, they will not be forgotten, and He will sweep away their sins as the morning mist is "burned off" by the sun. He called to them therefore to return to Him, "for I have redeemed you" (vv. 21ff.). Can the pieces of gold and wood converted into gods match that?

2. Idols are lifeless, do-nothing deities that have to be *carried* about, but the Lord is the living God who has *carried* His own people since their inception as a nation (see esp. 46:1-4).

Someone named Cyrus (a Mede) would issue an edict that Jews might return to their land, and that meant there would be political changes in Babylon. Implicit in Isaiah's prophecy is the knowledge that Medes and Persians would replace the Babylonians at the seat of power, and the citizenry would have to flee for their lives. The Babylonian gods might seem all-powerful; but when Cyrus and his armies attack, the idols would be carried in haste as the people run from the conquering armies. Isaiah described the scene:

> Bel bows down, Nebo stoops low;[4]
>   their idols are borne by beasts of burden.
> The images that are carried about are burdensome,
>   a burden for the weary.
>> (v. 1)

Picture the fleeing Babylonians. In their haste to get away they take only what is most important and treasured. They grab their images of wood and metal. But the idols are heavy, and their route leads through deep waters. The prophet continued his satire:

Lift up your skirts, bare your legs,
    and wade through the streams.
Your nakedness will be exposed
    and your shame uncovered.

(47:2-3)

Why don't the images help their worshipers? Of all the times when they could be helpful, surely this is the most urgent.

Picture the Israelites.

. . . You whom I have upheld since you were conceived,
    and have carried since your birth.
Even to your old age and gray hairs
    I am he, I am he who will sustain you.
I have made you and I will carry you;
    I will sustain you and I will rescue you.

(46:3-4)

The Lord had carried Israel out of Egypt (Exod. 19:4). The waters parted so the people could pass through and escape from Pharaoh. Now from exile He would carry them again and rescue them from captivity. The contrast between the Lord and the idols should not be missed: "Is there any God besides me? No, there is no other Rock; I know not one" (Isa. 44:8).

3. Idols are speechless and cannot predict the future, but the Lord has known the end from the beginning and has revealed His will to His people (see esp. 41:21-29; 44:24-28).

Although idols have mouths and lips—remember they are made in the likeness of humans (44:13)—they cannot communicate. They cannot tell what has happened or what will occur in the future (41:22f.). How then can they be called "gods"? With great sarcasm the Lord called to the images:

Do something, whether good or bad,
    so that we will be dismayed and filled with fear.
But you are less than nothing
    and your works are utterly worthless.

(41:23-24)

God, on the other hand, can and will predict the future, even events in the distant future (41:25ff.; 44:28; 45:1ff.). He will use a man named Cyrus to send the Jews back to Israel. Cyrus will do all of God's will, acting as His shepherd and His anointed, in behalf of God's chosen people. But God will order events of history so that the king will unknowingly act as His shepherd and His anointed (45:28; 46:1, 4, 5).

In a beautifully constructed poem, the Lord makes the case for His being the only true God (44:24ff.). He begins by claiming to be the Creator of everything in heaven and earth. By this He sets Himself apart from idols. He continues by revealing that false prophets are under His control and He makes fools of them. He makes light also of the wisdom of this world by turning it into nonsense. He is not subject to humans but is able to do with them as He pleases.

The Lord's prophets will see their words fulfilled. Such prophecies are not the vague and ambiguous mouthings of pagan oracles or the self-serving pronouncements of courtiers who speak only what they think the king wants to hear. They are quite clear and specific. Notice what God predicted: Jerusalem will be rebuilt from ruins; the temple once again restored. The city will be inhabited, not by an alien seed, but by the people who have been living in Babylon and are now to be sent back by Cyrus. Although the gods could not dry up the rivers for the fleeing Babylonians, the Lord will do that very thing for His people as they make their return.

Clearly, the Jews have nothing to fear from idols. But they should fear the Lord who has chosen them and has determined to bless them, even though they have often turned away from Him. We are to draw a similar conclusion from these facts. Even though images do not dominate Western culture, spiritual idolatry is rampant. But the gods we create and then pursue cannot help us. Our worship of them can only bring judgment upon us. We have the choice between the gods we make or the God who made us.

God's Case Against the Wicked
Against Nations

God deals with human beings as groups (families, nations) as well as individuals. In many passages, Scripture speaks of His judging the nations (1 Sam. 2:10; Pss. 7; 75; 96; 98 to mention a few). The major prophets have extended sections presenting God's case against the peoples of the countries surrounding Israel (Isa. 13-23; Jer. 46-51; Ezek. 25-32). These judgments have been carried out in history, although some predictions may seem to await complete fulfillment.

By using the image of a cup filled with judgment, many of the prophets predicted doom for those nations which had not acknowledged the Lord. In Jeremiah 25, the prophet foresaw the coming of Nebuchadnezzar against Judah, because the nation had not listened to His servants the prophets who had spoken prior to Jeremiah's time. There would be an exile of 70 years in Babylon, Jeremiah said. But then Babylon itself would be judged, "enslaved by many nations, and great kings" (v. 14). Then the prophetic vista broadened and the nations of the (then) world came into view:

> This is what the Lord, the God of Israel, said to me: Take from my hand this cup filled with the wine of my wrath and make all the nations. . . . stagger and go mad because of the sword I will send among them. (vv. 15-16)

A Bible atlas will enable the reader to see the extent of God's judgment. Some locations may not be clear (e.g., Buz and Zimri), but the effect of the enumeration is to see the vast extent of the judgment Jeremiah was proclaiming. The picture is one of each nation passing the cup to its neighbor, beginning with Judah and ending with Sheshach (Babylon).

God was determined to judge, and there was no way for the nations to avoid it. Jeremiah made this clear in verses 27-28:

> "Drink, get drunk and vomit, and fall to rise no more because of the sword I will send among you." But if they refuse to take the cup from your hand and drink, tell them, "This is what the Lord Almighty says: 'You must drink it.'"

The smaller nations of that time felt the wrath of God as they were conquered and made vassals to the empires on the march. The empires, too, experienced judgment, as one after the other was toppled by another more powerful. Clearly, Israel's God was the judge of all the earth.

But Jeremiah's vision seems to go beyond the events of that time. He predicted a time when "those slain by the Lord will be everywhere—from one end of the earth to the other. They will not be mourned or gathered up or buried, but will be like refuse lying on the ground" (v. 33). Isaiah saw a similar time (66:24), and John had a vision of it in Revelation (19:17ff.). A fearful expectation of judgment constantly haunts the nations of the world.

This judgment of the nations will grow out of the indictment God laid against them. Of course, they have broken God's law, and the wages of sin is death. But there are indications in Scripture that God has a special charge to lay against the nations: the world has abused, not helped, His people when they have been in need. Of all the nations surrounding Israel, the Bible singles out Edom as guilty of this, for the Edomites abused God's people more than once. As Israel approached Canaan, Moses asked the Edomites for permission to pass through their territory (Num. 20:14ff.). Edom refused, not once but twice. And since God had forbidden them to fight with Edom, Israel had no choice but to take a longer route.

Much later, Ezekiel spoke of Edom's sinful attitude at the time of Babylon's invasion. The Edomites "took revenge on the house of Judah" (25:12) and "harbored an ancient hostility and delivered the Israelites over to the sword at the time of their calamity" (35:5). Obadiah (vv. 8ff.) and Psalm 137:7 probably refer to the same events. This wicked attitude can be traced back to Esau himself (Gen. 27:41), and its progression can be seen in the refusal to permit Israel to pass through the land (mentioned in the paragraph above), in the treachery of Doeg the Edomite (cf. 1 Sam. 21; Ps. 52), the rebellion in the time of Jehoram, son of Jehoshaphat (2 Kings 8:20), the plots "against those you [the Lord] cherish" (recorded in Ps. 83:3ff.), and in the acts of violence mentioned by Joel (3:19) and Amos (1:11). Because of this unrelenting hostility toward God's people, Edom may stand as "a symbol of all the enemies of God and His people."[5]

It was for this special reason—their failure to help God's people when aid was requested as well as their open hostility in times of warfare—that God's wrath fell on the Edomites. The Book of Lamentations predicted that

> to you also the cup will be passed;
>> you will be drunk and stripped naked.
>>
>> (4:21)

Jeremiah foresaw Edom's fall (49:7ff.), and Malachi its perpetual curse (1:2-5). The judgment came to pass when Edom was driven out of its mountainous territory by Nabatean Arabs sometime after 500 B.C. Only occasionally do individuals trace their lineage to Esau; the most infamous, Herod the Great.

Isaiah had a vision of one coming from Edom where He had stained His clothing with the blood of His adversaries (63:1). His triumph over Edom symbolized redemption for His people (v. 4). Here, clearly, we have a reference to Edom as the exemplar of all nations who reject Christ and persecute His people. (Note once again the reference to drinking the cup in v. 6). And what Isaiah saw was revealed also to John, who recorded his vision in Revelation 19. The time of this judgment coincides with the deliverance of God's people.

All this is evidence of God's jealous care for His own. The same thought is evident in Jesus' prediction of the judgment for the sheep and the goats (Matt. 25:31). When He returns, all nations will stand before Him. He will separate them with sheep on His right and goats on His left. His blessing will rest on the sheep because they cared for Him when He was in need. When sheep protest that they were never aware of doing this for Him, He replies, ". . . whatever you did for one of the least of these brothers of mine, you did for me" (v. 40). On the other hand, His judgment will rest on the goats because they did not help Him when He was in need. When goats protest that they were never aware of neglecting Him, He replies, ". . . whatever you did not do for one of the least of these, you did not do for me" (v. 45). The judgment sends them "into the eternal fire prepared for the devil and his angels" (v. 41). What a dreadful thing God's judgment is! And to think that He cares so much for His own in this world that such a judgment falls on those who mistreat the people of God.

These judgments fall upon nations for their wicked deeds. Of course, should individuals within these nations disown such evil and embrace the Lord's offer of salvation, they would certainly escape the judgment. Rahab, Ruth, the centurion of Matthew 8—all these were exempt from the judgment that fell on Canaan, Moab, and Rome, respectively.

Against Individuals

The case against sinful individuals was first made against Adam and Eve (Gen. 3:16ff.), and the judgment was carried out soon thereafter (vv. 23f.). Something of the vehemence behind God's act of judgment can be seen in the words used to describe the expulsion from the garden—"banished" and "drove out." The latter phrase in Hebrew is used in other parts of the Old Testament to describe a forceful and vigorous driving out. Consider Cain's words, "Today you are *driving* me out from the land" (Gen. 4:14), or Sarah's jealous words to Abraham when she saw Ishmael mocking her son, "*Get rid of* that slave woman" (21:10). (In commenting on this latter event, Paul used the term "cast out" [Gal. 4:30, KJV], the same word in Greek used to describe Jesus' purifying the temple [Matt. 21:12 and parallel passages in the other Gospels].) Moses and Aaron felt the rage of Pharaoh when he refused to answer their plea to let the people go: "they were *driven out* of Pharaoh's presence" (Exod. 10:11). David said, "They have now *driven* me from my share in the Lord's inheritance" (1 Sam. 26:19). He said this when Saul and three thousand chosen men pursued him to lynch him, because Saul knew that David was preferred before him.

Clearly Adam and Eve were not receiving a gentle send-off. "Banished" is a good way to express it. According to Paul, this banishment (and the spiritual death that accompanied it) passed on to all of Adam's race (Rom. 5:12ff.). That is why Jesus said, "... whoever does not believe stands condemned already" (John 3:18). In a sense, the case has been made against unbelievers and the judgment already passed. (Consider similar words made concerning Satan in John 16:11.) That is why there is such urgency in preaching the Gospel. Unless human beings believe, their judgment has already been decided.

This judgment explains the trouble in the world. Many would deny the existence of God because of catastrophes in the world. Scriptures turn the reasoning around and claim that rebellion on the part of human beings is the reason for our misery:

> The wrath of God is being revealed from heaven against all the godlessness and wickedness of men who suppress the truth by their wickedness. (Rom. 1:18)

There is an old adage, "Be sure your sin will find you out." The statement is defective since it leaves God out. Far better it is to speak of His present providential rule over the earth and to use an expression frequently found in the Old Testament: God "will bring down on his [the sinner's] head what he has done" (1 Kings 8:31; see also Ps. 7:16; Ezek. 9:10 et al.; Joel 3:4, 7; Obad. 15). Keil paraphrases 1 Kings 8:31 this way: "to cause the merited punishment to fall upon him."[6] In God's providence we often see a continuing judgment on those who rebel against His way.

Thus the judgment of God may be viewed as past or as on-going. It is also a future reality whose certainty in Scripture is never doubted: ". . . a fearful expectation of judgment and of raging fire that will consume the enemies of God" (Heb. 10:27). Some of the biblical facts about judgment may be summarized as follows:

- Judgment has been committed to Jesus, the victorious Messiah. (John 5:24ff.)
- Judgment is in response to sins. (Eph. 5:5f.; Col. 3:5f.)
- Judgment rests on God's omniscience and His justice. (Rom. 2:2, 6; cf. Ps. 62:12)
- Judgment will come at the end of the world and with the appearance of the new heaven and earth. (Rev. 20:11ff.)

God's Case Against His Own People

The Christians in Ephesus rejoiced to receive the letter from John, and they listened eagerly as it was being read to them. They were excited to hear about the vision he had seen on Patmos, and they became ecstatic when told that Jesus Himself wanted the scroll sent to them. It was a real comfort to know that He walked among the churches and even held their "angel" in His right hand. So when the reader came to the part especially addressed to "the angel of the church in Ephesus," the Ephesian Christians leaned forward to catch every word.

They were delighted that the risen Lord found so much to commend them for. After all, they suffered much and still kept the faith. They defended the faith against the Nicolaitans, whose practices they had learned to hate. But then they heard the chilling and sobering words. "Yet I hold this against you" (Rev. 2:4). The Son of God was laying a charge against them: they had forsaken their first love. He would accuse them now, like a prosecuting attorney. He would be their judge later if they did not repent.

The Ephesian church was not the only congregation to be indicted. The Savior accused other churches in Asia Minor with different charges from those He brought against the Ephesians (cf. 2:14, 20; 3:1ff., 15ff.).

The letters of the Apocalypse made clear that the Lord sometimes acts as lawyer, prosecuting His own people when they stray from Him. Of course, this was not the first time that God had to accuse His people. He often did so during the wilderness journey and during the period of the judges. However, it was left to the prophets to make detailed indictments (cf. Jer. 2:9, 29; Hos. 4:1; 12:2; Mic. 6:1ff.).

Reading through the prophets, one is impressed that Israel sinned not against one point of the law only but against each single commandment. Moreover, the Israelites were guilty of hypocrisy, they retained the proper forms of worship even though their hearts were not in them. What brought about this state of affairs? The prophets claimed that an unbelievable thing had happened, and they called upon inanimate creation to hear the charge and be appalled (Jer. 2:12; Mic. 6:1f.). God's people had become weary of Him, of keeping His law, and of maintaining their uniqueness in the world. The Lord asked a series of rhetorical questions of His people, spread over the periods in which the prophets testified:

> What more could have been done for my vineyard
>   than I have done for it?
>
>   (Isa. 5:4)

> My people, what have I done to you?
>   How have I burdened you?
>
>   (Mic. 6:3)

> What fault did your fathers find in me,
>   that they strayed so far from me?
>
>   (Jer. 2:5)

Malachi made it very explicit:

> "But you profane it by saying of the Lord's table, 'It is defiled,' and of its food, 'It is contemptible.' And you say, 'What a burden!' and you sniff at it contemptuously," says the Lord Almighty. (Mal. 1:12f.)

In the course of time, the excitement of being God's people, the amazement of His grace toward them, and the incomparable honor of bearing His name—all these seemed as nothing in comparison with what heathen idols and their religions offered. Belonging to God had become a great big bore, and the hearts of God's people found their treasures elsewhere. The desire to be like other nations (1 Sam. 8:5, 20), which began in the political arena, now extended to every part of their lives. Peer pressure had triumphed over history, making God and His way irrelevant.

This charge against Israel was the same as God's indictment of the Ephesian Christians: they had forsaken their first love (Rev. 2:4). As Swete aptly writes, "The new Israel had begun too soon to follow the example of the ancient people of God."[7] In a sense, the Ephesian error lies at the root of other sins. Perhaps that is why Jesus spoke of their sin with such vehemence: "you have forsaken your first love" and "you have fallen" from a great height (vv. 4f.).

Half-heartedness does not usually shock us, but God judges it harshly. In the days of Jeremiah, when comparing half-hearted Judah with openly wicked Israel, He said:

> I gave faithless Israel her certificate of divorce and sent her away because of all her adulteries. Yet I saw that her unfaithful sister Judah had no fear; she also went out and committed adultery. Because Israel's immorality mattered so little to her, she defiled the land and committed adultery with stone and wood. In spite of all this, her unfaithful sister Judah did not return to me with all her heart, but only in pretense. . . . Faithless Israel is more righteous than unfaithful Judah. (Jer. 3:8-11)

God was here making a comparison between the two nations of the covenant. He said, in effect, I would rather have honest unbelief than hypocritical orthodoxy. He made the same judgment regarding the Laodiceans:

> I know your deeds, that you are neither cold nor hot. I wish you were either one or the other! So, because you are lukewarm—neither hot nor cold—I am about to spit you out of my mouth. (Rev. 3:15f.)

Hypocrisy is not only a root of many other transgressions, it is high on the list of those things which are repulsive to a holy God. The cure for hypocrisy is to "repent and do the things you did at first" (Rev. 2:4). There is something refreshing about the life of a young Christian. "I remember the devotion of your youth, how as a bride you loved me and followed me through the desert" (Jer. 2:2). If only we could preserve that devotion all our lives and not allow the things of God to become common. But the people of God throughout their long history in both testaments all too frequently fell into such a reprehensible habit.

God's Defense of His Saints and the Church

In a vision Zechariah the prophet saw his associate Joshua, the high priest, standing before the Lord and about to be accused by Satan (3:1ff.). The prophet had already seen visions both of the overthrow of those nations which had scattered Israel throughout the world of that time and of the restoration of His people to the land and to His favor. He was to be shown just how God, who had been angry with the Jews, could now be so kind and merciful in His relations with them.

Zechariah saw Joshua as a prisoner "in the dock." Joshua was not being judged for individual sin but stood in his official capacity as a representative of the nation. This was most appropriate. Since Israel was to be a "royal priesthood," in the absence of a true king the high priest was the embodiment of national identity. Satan was there as the accuser of the saints, standing at Joshua's right hand.

But before the trial could get under way, Satan was rebuked by the Lord. He might be tolerated in God's presence, but he had no official standing. Something of the vehemence of God's action can be gathered by studying the use of the word *rebuke* in the Bible. God rebuked the Red Sea. Jesus rebuked the winds of Galilee, the Devil, demons, fevers attacking the people, and Peter when he expressed the wish that Jesus would not go to the cross. Moreover, Satan had done the unthinkable: he "brought a charge against those whom God has chosen" (Rom. 8:33). So, "The Lord, who has chosen Jerusalem, rebuke you, Satan" (Zech. 3:2). God, in His eternal plan, had determined to bless His people, and Satan would never be allowed to thwart that purpose.

In addition, the people of God had already been judged for their sins. They were a burning stick, snatched from the fire of the exile. Purged by their suffering, they were now ready for a new development in God's purposes for them. But that suffering, severe as it was, could never remove the filth of their sin. We next see the priest as he and the nation really appeared to God. The word "filthy" refers to human excrement smeared over Joshua's garments. Not only unclean ceremonially and socially, the high priest was revolting and repulsive. Clearly, something had to be done.

The Lord, seen here as the Angel of the Lord (v. 1), proceeded to announce Joshua's justification and renewal. "Take off his filthy clothes. . . . I have taken away your sin" (v. 4; cf. 2 Sam. 12:13; 24:10). This was not the decree of a sovereign acting in disregard of the law but of a judge upholding the law. Preoccupied with sacrifices and ceremonies, Joshua would have understood how this cleansing might be done: by the shedding of blood of a clean animal offered by a penitent sinner.

"And I will put rich garments on you" (cf. Exod. 28). Zechariah participated in the vision he was seeing and asked that the priestly turban be placed on the high priest's head (Exod. 28:36ff.). The most significant part of the turban was the gold plate attached to it. The plate bore the inscription "Holy to the Lord. . . . It will be on Aaron's forehead continually so that they will be acceptable to the Lord."

With these acts Joshua was fully reinvested with the symbolism of his office, and the nation was now ready for its new place in the kingdom of God. Obedience would be a condition of future blessing (Zech. 3:6f.). In His providence the Lord would bring the Messiah ("my servant, the Branch") and His kingdom ("the stone"), and the sin would be removed in one day. Joshua's sin had been taken away in view of the once-for-all removal that would take place at Calvary.

This courtroom scene, under rich Old Testament symbolism, illustrates God's judgment for every child of His. Sin, offensive and disgusting as it is to a righteous God, has been put away and our accuser thoroughly rebuked. Paul put it this way:

> He forgave us all our sins, having canceled the written code, with its regulations, that was against us and that stood opposed to us; he took it away, nailing it to the cross. And having disarmed the powers and authorities, he made a public spectacle of them, triumphing over them by the cross. (Col. 2:13-15)

In addition, alien righteousness has been imputed to us so that it is really ours. And we are now ready to participate in God's program for redemption in the world.

But God's judicial acts in behalf of His own people do not cease with such acts of reinstatement. He continues to rise to our defense. He heard David's plea in Psalm 35:1:

> Contend, O Lord, with those who contend with me.
> (cf. Isa. 49:25)

In particular, God defends the defenseless, fatherless, widows, the needy, and the poor (Ps. 140:12; Prov. 22:22f.; 23:11 and many others).

Sometimes vindication seems slow in coming. Micah 7:7, 9 speaks of this, as the prophet foresaw the exile and put himself in the place of faithful deportees who awaited the promised return patiently:

> But as for me, I watch in hope for the Lord,
>   I wait for God my Savior;
>   my God will hear me. . . .
> Because I have sinned against him,
>   I will bear the Lord's wrath,
> until he pleads my case
>   and establishes my right.

This is the confidence of all who are unjustly treated. God has a timetable for them, but He will surely keep His promise.

Something of the continual defense of His people may be seen in the brief conversation between Jesus and Peter just after the Last Supper (Luke 22). Peter and the others had been debating about who was the greatest disciple among them. In response Jesus pulled aside the curtain hiding the unseen world and told Peter of an event there that would affect him greatly:

> Simon, Simon, Satan has asked to sift you [plural] as wheat. But I have prayed for you [singular], Simon, that your faith may not fail. (vv. 31-32)

Although the entire group needed protection, Jesus singled out Peter because He was talking to him. Just when Satan was permitted to petition before the throne of God for freedom to tempt Peter, Jesus was there to defend His disciple. Satan's request was granted, but so was Jesus'! Peter would be tempted, but through it all he would have the assurance of ultimate recovery and usefulness: "And when you have turned back, strengthen your brothers" (v. 32). We all must wonder how often such a scene is repeated in reference to each of us as Satan continues his requests, and Jesus our advocate continues His defense of us (1 John 2:1).

The trial of Joshua may not be unlike the final judgment John saw in his vision (Rev. 20:11ff.). It is true that Satan was no longer there, for he had already been judged (v. 10). But the books certainly contained the records of each person's works. Those whose names were not written in the Book of Life were judged, and we may infer that those whose names were written in it were granted entrance into the new Jerusalem. Their sins were not ignored; their names were in the book of the Lamb, the one who had been offered for their sins and had freed them from their sins by His blood (cf. 1:6).

No, we need not fear God's justice when He is at our side to defend us. In fact, we may take the greatest of comfort from it. No wonder the old saint mentioned at the beginning of this chapter could face her own death in such peace.

Notes

[1] The images of judge and lawyer overlap in Scripture, so that it is not usually worthwhile to distinguish between them.

[2] Konig aptly calls God's indictment of idols, "mocking the gods." See his *Here Am I!*, 1ff.

[3] *The Anchor Bible: Hosea*, 219.

[4] *Bel* and *Nebo* are names of Babylonian gods.

[5] *The NIV Study Bible*, 1064. Because of this symbolic character of Edom, Ellison argues that the prophecy against it is properly placed in Ezekiel 36: "So before Ezekiel turns to the accomplishment of God's purpose with His land and people [i.e., in chaps. 36ff.] he solemnly foretells judgment on all those, who having gone their own way like Edom, hate the people of God and seek to deprive them of what is theirs by God's giving" (*Ezekiel: The Man and His Message*, 124).

[6] *The Books of the Kings*, 129.

[7] *The Apocalypse of St. John*, 26.

20. Farmer

Our family used to spend several weeks each summer on a farm in western Maryland, and I can still recall the feeling of admiration as I watched the farmer at his work. During any week he would be a mechanic, an electrician, a carpenter, a hunter, a salesman, and a curer of hams in the smokehouse. He had to know about vegetables and fruits, their diseases and pests, and when to plant and how often to weed. He understood animal husbandry, acting as dietician, midwife, and veterinarian for his horses, mules, cattle, pigs, chickens, and sheep. On occasion he would repair his telephone lines so he could speak with the outside world—and the other 15 parties on the same line! Truly, to a boy growing up in the city, a farmer was something else again. We should have no less a sense of awe when we think of God as farmer.

Isaiah 5

Isaiah wrote a poem about God and His vineyard, Judah (chap. 5). The land was fertile, and God did all that was needed for the vines to yield good grapes. He plowed the soil, clearing away the stones as well as the stratum of rocks just below the surface. He planted the best vines, then waited for the time of grapes. He had to wait patiently for at least two years. While waiting, He built a tower (perhaps of the stones He had removed)

172

to spy out predatory beasts, and He cut a trough in the ground to gather the juice of the winepress. Because He had spared no expense or effort to have the best of vineyards, His expectations were very high. "But it yielded only bad [other possible translations here are "wild," "stinking," "worthless"] fruit" (v. 2).

God's first reaction was amazement: "What more could I have done . . . ? why did it yield only bad [grapes]?" (v. 4; cf. Jer. 2:21). The divine farmer had left no stone unturned in preparing the land, and He had planted the best of vines. As Peter put it, "His divine power has given us everything we need for life and godliness" (2 Pet. 1:3). No one can ever blame God for short-comings in the Christian life. It must always be amazing that we don't take full advantage of our salvation.

The amazement is all the more understandable when we consider that "the men of Judah are the garden of his delight" (v. 7). God's preparation of the land and His care for the vines had not been drudgery. Rather, the work was a labor of love lavished on His people because He derived such pleasure from them. That a righteous God could delight in such a people over so many years is a token of His amazing grace. That they could be so unresponsive to all His goodness is a testimony to the perversity and tenacity of sin.

But His wonderment soon changed to anger. He would not just abandon the useless vineyard, He would destroy it. This meant that God would take away the protecting hedge, break down the walls so that animals could devour the fruit, make the vineyard a wasteland, and forbid rain to fall on it.

Isaiah's song covers many centuries of Israel's history. The farmer is not a rash, hot-headed person who becomes upset over one year's crop failure. Israel had been planted for hundreds of years, and the fruit had been worthless much of the time. When we compare the grace exhibited over the years with the miserable results, we sense God's disappointment and the end of His long-suffering.

One lesson we should draw from Isaiah's prophecy is that God has every right to expect and demand fruit from His creatures. Paul cited this as a truism in 2 Timothy 2:6: "The hardworking farmer should be the first to receive a share of the crops" (cf. also 1 Cor. 9:10ff.). Fruitfulness is a proof of salvation; holiness is not an option for the child of God. If in the physical world the farmer has the right to expect to reap what he has sown, so God has the right to expect justice and righteousness in the lives of His children.

Jesus said that the Father "cuts off every branch in me that bears no fruit, while every branch that does bear fruit he prunes so that it will be even more fruitful" (John 15:2). There can be nothing more important in a Christian's life than the fruit he or she can produce for God. It is more important than job, happiness, or influence. Such things may be sacrificed if only we bear fruit.

A second lesson is that not just any fruit will do. God looked for good grapes (Isa. 5:4), so why did the vine yield something foreign and repulsive? He looked for justice and righteousness (v. 7), so why did Israel bear bloodshed and cries of distress?[1] The rest of Isaiah 5 gives us examples of the worthless fruit produced by Judah. The people were greedy (v. 8), given to drunkenness (vv. 11ff., 22), deceitful (vv. 18ff.), mockers (v. 20), and perverse (v. 23). Such selfishness was directed against the poor of the land who suffered bloodshed and distress (v. 7). Abuse of fellow human beings is bad fruit in the eyes of God. We may not offer to God what the world thinks is good or even what the Christian community might be willing to settle for. We must produce and offer to Him what He cherishes and has designated as "good grapes."

A third lesson is that the farmer will not long put up with unproductive vineyards and fields. Although He may be long-suffering and sometimes persuaded to defer judgment (Luke 13:6ff.), His patience should not be allowed to lull us into a state of complacency. Sooner or later He will make the fruitless area a wasteland.

Psalm 80

By the time Asaph was writing Psalm 80, Isaiah's prediction had come true. Asaph seemed to recall Isaiah 5 when he spoke of God's bringing a vine from Egypt, driving out the nations of Canaan, planting the vine after clearing the ground. The vine took root and spread throughout the land (vv. 8-10). But now the vineyard was unprotected; boars and creatures of the field ravaged it. The vines had been cut down and burned in the fire. The poet utters the significant words, "... at your rebuke your people perish" (v. 16). Aware of God's sovereign control over history, Asaph could not but attribute Israel's destruction to God and His anger.

Since God had in the past lavished such loving care on the vine, Asaph had cause for trusting that God would return to His vine in the future. The farmer cannot easily give up his land. Note the names by which the psalmist addresses the Lord: "Shepherd of Israel," the one who sits "enthroned between the cherubim [over the ark of the covenant]," "Lord God Almighty." These are time-honored expressions of God's power, His intense concern for the people He had chosen, and His grace and long-suffering. Surely God would make His face shine upon them again (v. 19), and Aaron's benediction would once again be a reality (Num. 6:22ff.).

So it is not surprising that Isaiah foresaw the day when God's care for His vineyard would be revived at the same time that Leviathan, the sea monster symbolic of evil nations, would be destroyed (30:2ff.). Israel would once again take root, bud, and blossom, filling the earth with fruit. God would once again water His vineyard continually and guard it against predatory animals day and night. No longer would He be angry with the plants. He would be angry against briers and thorns that might threaten the grapes. If such growth became a danger, people would see how fierce He could become in protecting His vines!

Here we see a fundamental principle of God's attitude toward His elect. He does not long forsake them but responds quickly to their repentance:

> For a brief moment I abandoned you [70 years],
> > but with deep compassion I will bring you back.
> In a surge of anger
> > I hid my face from you for a moment,
> but with everlasting kindness
> > I will have compassion on you.
> > > > > (Isa. 54:7-8)

Jesus' Parables

Although no record shows that Jesus engaged in farming of any kind, His teachings are full of agricultural illustrations. In Mark 3, Jesus' actions had so raised the anger of Pharisees and Herodians (who were usually not allies) that they conspired together to kill Him (v. 6). Even his family, His mother and brothers, thought He was out of His mind (v. 21). Soon after, teachers of the law accused Him of consorting with demons, a charge that could carry the death penalty (v. 23). Surely His ministry, so successful at the start, was now being seen as a failure. How could He possibly succeed?

Jesus' response to all these accusations and schemings was the parable of the sower. He would succeed in the same way that a farmer would succeed. Sure, some seed would fall by the wayside and never germinate; some would be scorched by the sun before it had taken root; some would take root but later be choked by thorns and yield nothing. But the greater part of the seed would fall upon good soil and produce an unusually large harvest. It would succeed where other things would fail. Jesus had great faith in His Word!

His disciples have not always taken this lesson to heart. Too often, God's people turned to Assyria or Egypt for help rather than counting on the power of Scripture. They went into exile for their trouble. The record of church history is one of alliances with political powers rather than of obedience to the Bible, and many saints have suffered deeply because of these entangling alliances. Yet Jesus stands by His Word: "He who has ears to hear, let him hear" (v. 9).

In another parable associated with that of the sower (Matt. 13:24), Jesus teaches us that Satan also is active as a farmer. He sows weeds, the kind that cannot be easily distinguished from wheat when young. If one were to try to weed out Satan's crops, the good wheat would be rooted up with them. As a farmer, Satan sows and then looks for results; the worthless and perhaps poisonous plants serve his purpose to deceive and to destroy.

Christians can be deceived by the weeds, especially in their early stages of growth. I recall a young man who started coming to our church and immediately threw himself into every activity of the congregation. He was present at every meeting, eager to help with distributing hymnals and seeing that everyone was comfortable. He joined in the prayer meeting and seemed earnest in Bible study. He was just the kind of young person any pastor would welcome into the fellowship. After a month we saw no more of him. I looked him up, but he had lost interest. We talked about God and His claims, but he didn't care. Then the full story came out. Just prior to coming to our church, he had committed adultery. Feeling deeply ashamed, he was working off his guilt by church attendance. When the sense of guilt eventually passed, the reason for being at church evaporated. I continued to hope that the fellow would be soundly converted, but we never saw him again.

One of the lessons of this parable is that we should be on the watch for the appearance of weeds. We should not engage in witch hunts, suspecting everyone of being false; but we should be realistic, knowing that Satan is active in sowing his seed. Also, when the weeds become apparent we should not be discouraged. These things happen as part of the warfare we are engaged in. We have a wise (but not omniscient) enemy, a powerful (but not omnipotent) foe. At harvest time, at the end of the world, God will make an infallible judgment to separate the wheat and the weeds. Meantime, they grow together.

Up to this point in our study we have seen God as the solitary farmer who works the land for His own particular advantage. In three other parables in Matthew, the image shifts to that of a landowner who employs hired workers to do the daily labor in the vineyard. But it should be pointed out that the landowner is no less interested in the vineyard simply because he doesn't do the actual work in the parable. The vineyard is still the foremost concern in his mind.

In the parable of the workers (Matt. 20:1ff.), the landowner hires men at different times of the day but all at the same wage. So, at evening, each laborer receives the agreed-upon amount. Those who had worked longer grumbled at this supposed inequity. The landowner reasoned with them that they got what they had agreed to and, further, that he had the right to do what he wanted with his own money. "Or are you envious because I am generous?" (v. 15).

This reasoning sounds strange to modern ears, but it only goes to show that God's thoughts are not always our thoughts. The kingdom of God does not have a labor contract for its workers. In fact, the kingdom of God is based throughout on grace, with no place for merit. In the kingdom of God there are no rights (after all, didn't we lose our rights when we sinned?). Instead, we find instances of God's generosity. There are rewards for service and for faithfulness, but they are calculated not by human standards. That is why "the last will be first, and the first will be last" (v. 16).

But faithfulness and sincerity in a good cause do bring their rewards. In Matthew 21:28 and following, the landowner sent his two sons out to work for him in the vineyard. One at first refused to do so, but then changed his mind. The other showed more respect; "I will, sir," he said, but then didn't. Jesus asked the chief priests and elders to whom he had addressed this parable, "Which of the two did what his father wanted?" When He had heard their reply, He applied the parable directly to them. John the Baptist preached the way of righteousness to the Jewish leaders and to the despised prostitutes and tax collectors. Jewish leaders had always paid God lip-service with their long prayers and their widely publicized gifts to the treasury, but they did not produce the kind of obedience John demanded of them (Matt. 3:7ff.). They had said, "I will," but then didn't. The blatant sinners, on the other hand, had not obeyed John. They continued with their prostitution and their cheating as tax collectors. Yet when Jesus finally spoke to them, they left their evil ways and followed him (Matt. 9:9ff.; Luke 7:36ff.; 19:1ff.). The parable enforces the biblical principle that hypocrisy does not impress God; indeed, its reward is a stiff judgment. But repentance, even if at first refused, gives entrance into the kingdom of God.

In Matthew 21, Jesus seemed to be adapting Isaiah's parable to His own day. God is again the landowner who plants a vineyard (vv. 33ff.). He prepares it and then rents it out to farmers while he himself goes away on a journey. This time there is no question of bad fruit. There is fruit all right, but the landowner doesn't collect because those he sends to the farmers are beaten, killed, and stoned. The tenants are truly "wretches" (v. 41). They even kill the landowner's son when he is sent, showing their total contempt for the landowner and for the son he thought they would respect.

As in Isaiah, the central truth is the importance of returning to God the fruit He has provided for. He has the right to it, but His rights are not considered. Have you noticed how often in this day of civil rights, human rights, states' rights, and the Bill of Rights no one even thinks of God's rights? In Jesus' day it was the same. God was so far removed from people's day-by-day thinking that His creatorship was ignored and denied in every practical way.

Satan knows exactly what he is doing when he dupes people into denying and ignoring the doctrine of creation. If God did create, then the world is His (Ps. 24:1), and we are trespassers if we disobey His law. Of course, if He did not create, then He is an interloper, and we have nothing to fear from Him.

But the parable of the wicked tenants does teach accountability and reinforces what we have already seen: God expects, and has the right to expect, returns from those who dwell on His green earth. When this expectation is denied, as in both Isaiah's and Matthew's accounts, God's anger is aroused. Interestingly His reaction is quite a normal one. Jesus asked His hearers what the landowner should do to the greedy tenants. Not realizing that He was speaking of them, they responded:

> He will bring those wretches to a wretched end, . . . and he will rent the vineyard to other tenants, who will give him his share of the crop at harvest time. (Matt. 21:41)

Foolish people! They know quite well what *they* would do under similar circumstances, but it never occurs to them that *God* should do the same thing. The leaders have such a mistaken idea of God that they cannot conceive He has an interest in His world and His creatures. When Jesus applied the parable to Himself as the son of the landowner and to the Jews as the tenants by quoting Psalm 118:22-24, the light dawned. Then they tried to do away with Him, but His popularity at that moment forestalled any such effort.

But the return from the vineyard is so important to the owner that he says he will give the vineyard to others. This is a reference to the Gentiles, who now have the privilege, and the responsibility, of producing fruit acceptable to God and giving it to Him.

As farmer, God has rights. That is the first lesson. He has the right to receive the crops, the right to receive faithful service from His employees, and the right to reward His workers as He will. This truth emphasized throughout the agricultural pictures in the Bible also shows God's personal interest in spreading the kingdom. He is concerned to guide Arcturus through the galaxy, but He has a major interest in His kingdom on earth. In that kingdom there are no favorites, for all labor by grace and in grace. Moreover, if the tenants fail in their responsibility, they can easily be replaced (Matt. 3:9).

A second lesson has to do with those parables which speak of bad, or unacceptable, fruit growing on the vines. As we have seen, God cannot be blamed for this. The evil fruit comes from human depravity that so easily and so often turns away from God and seeks to thwart His ways. The solution lies in the willingness to pray that God would search the heart to

> see if there is any offensive way in me,
> and lead me in the way everlasting.
>
> (Ps. 139:24)

Notes
[1] As many commentators observe, Isaiah was punning here. The Hebrew words translated "justice" and "bloodshed" sound the same; so do those translated "righteousness" and "distress."

21. Potter

The Gospel accounts of the exorcism of the man from Gadara give us vivid pictures of the two very different states of that remarkable man. Before he met Jesus he:

> lived in the tombs, and no one could bind him any more, not even with a chain. For he had often been chained hand and foot, but he tore the chains apart and broke the irons on his feet. No one was strong enough to subdue him. Night and day among the tombs and in the hills he would cry out and cut himself with stones. (Mark 5:3-5)

What a tragic thing to happen to a human being who was God's image, whose progenitors had been formed by God in the Creation.

After Jesus had cast out the demon, the man was found "sitting there, dressed and in his right mind" (v. 15). Though not yet restored to the perfection known in Eden, the Gadarene had experienced a truly remarkable renovation that affected his whole being.

This event gives an illustration of the truth Jeremiah learned when God sent him to a potter's workshop in Jerusalem (Jer. 18:1ff.). The prophet watched as the potter worked at his wheel. Pottery shops were familiar sights in Jerusalem in those days, for their wares were much in demand. Clay utensils provided an excellent means for storing things. They were superior to baskets, for they held water as baskets could not and their contents were safe from hungry, scavenging animals. Clay pots were cheaper than metal containers, so even the poor possessed them.

The work required good clay, a wheel upon which it could be shaped, and the skillful and sensitive hands of a potter. As Jeremiah looked on, the pot on the wheel was "marred." The Hebrew word used here also appears in Genesis 6:11 where it describes the earth and the people who had corrupted it. The clay would no longer serve the purpose the potter originally had in mind. So he shaped it into another pot, "as it seemed best to him" (Jer. 18:4).

Jeremiah heard the Lord apply the lesson:

> "O house of Israel, can I not do with you as this potter does?" declares the Lord. "Like clay in the hand of the potter, so are you in my hand, O house of Israel." (18:6)

The people of Jerusalem were denying this fact. They thought that nothing could or would happen to them because of their past relationship with God. Jeremiah had told them that this was a lie (7:1ff.), but they had not listened to his warnings. Now their leaders could see vividly what God could do. If they listened to Jeremiah's announcements of destruction and repented of their covenant breaking, He would "relent and not inflict on it the disaster he had planned" (v. 8). The clay would then be shaped in accordance with the potter's original intention. But if, though blessings had been predicted, they disobeyed the Lord, He would "reconsider the good I had intended to do for it" (v. 10). The clay would be marred and would have to be used for another purpose.

This declaration clearly refuted their view that God's blessings came automatically. Had the people of Jeremiah's day read Leviticus 26 and Deuteronomy 28 they would have realized that covenant blessings are conditioned by obedience. Judgments are just as certain as blessings among a people whose God is the Lord.

The Lord continued His word to Jeremiah with a further

application of the figure of potter. Jerusalem was to hear once again of impending doom and of the opportunity to escape it (v. 11).[1] But instead of listening, the people proved themselves to be "marred clay." Note how the Lord described them:

> ... my people have forgotten me;
>   they burn incense to worthless idols,
> which made them stumble in their ways
>   and in the ancient paths.

(v. 15)

Instead of repenting, they planned to start a smear campaign against Jeremiah so that no one would listen to him (v. 18).

God's response called for the prophet to make another visit to a potter's shop, this time to buy a clay jar (19:1ff.). In the company of some of the leaders, Jeremiah went to the valley of the sons of Hinnom, just outside the walls of the city. Again, he predicted disaster for the city and its people. As he spoke, he smashed the pot he had just purchased as a sign of what the Lord would do:

> I will smash this nation and this city just as this potter's jar is smashed and cannot be repaired. (v. 11)

Through these events God was manifestly teaching His sovereignty over the people of Judah and His freedom to mold them as He would—for blessing if they were faithful to Him, for ill if they continued in their disobedience. We are not to infer that He is whimsical or changeable in His relations with them but that He acts according to His revealed plan for them. As Jeremiah would say years later when disaster did strike the city,

> The Lord has done what he planned;
>   he has fulfilled his word,
>   which he decreed long ago.

(Lam. 2:17)

In an earlier message through Isaiah the Lord had used the image of a potter to rebuke the people of Jerusalem for their hypocrisy (29:13ff.). Note that they had retained all the proper forms of religion (v. 13), but their hearts were not in their worship. In their hearts they had come to the conclusion that God could not save them from their enemies, and so the people of God had turned first to Assyria and then to Egypt for help. In all this scheming they did not seek God's counsel; in fact, they tried to hide their plans from Him. God's reaction was swift in coming:

> You turn things upside down,
>   as if the potter were thought to be like the clay!
> Shall what is formed say to him who formed it,
>   "He did not make me"?
> Can the pot say of the potter,
>   "He knows nothing"?
>
> (v. 16)

The leaders of Judah had forgotten that God must be God! They were treating Him as if He were just another finite being— one who could be offered false worship but who would not perceive their hypocrisy; one from whom the leaders could successfully hide their secret meetings to make alliances with foreign states; one whose wisdom was so suspect that it could be ignored with impunity and substituted with the leaders' own supposed superior thoughts.

These are the views of modern humanists, who not hypocritically but explicitly reject God, His omniscience, and His wisdom. They differ from ancient Israelites only in that they do not try to hide their disavowal of God. Whether hidden or open, these views are contradicted by Scripture. "Nothing in all creation is hidden from God's sight. Everything is uncovered and laid bare before the eyes of him to whom we must give account" (Heb. 4:13).

In questioning the wisdom of God, the Jewish leaders forgot what had been revealed in the Psalter when at another time wicked people were abusing their neighbors and saying, "The Lord does not see; the God of Jacob pays no heed" (Ps. 94:7).[2]

The psalmist argues, in response, that God the Creator cannot but know all things.

Take heed, you senseless ones among the people;
  you fools, when will you become wise?
Does he who implanted the ear not hear?
  Does he who formed the eye not see? . . .
The Lord knows the thoughts of man;
  he knows that they are futile.

(Ps. 94:8-11)

So when God reveals Himself as potter, He wants us to realize that the potter is not like the clay and cannot be treated that way. It is not only folly, it is blasphemy to do so. Nor can the clay, which has received its identity from the potter, ever declare its independence from him. Such thinking is also folly and blasphemy. And how can the clay ever think that the potter, who has given it its utility and beauty, knows nothing?

But because God is the potter and His people are only clay, their plans will not succeed, and God's will. The leaders were symbolized by Lebanon, whose trees would be destroyed leaving only uncultivated fields (Isa. 29:17a). These leaders would soon be gone along with the ruthless, the mockers, and those who use the courts not for justice but for their own selfish ends. But the deaf and blind, the humble and the needy, who have been abused by the ruling class, would rejoice in the Lord, for He would bless them so that they would be like a forest (29:17b).

In another passage from Isaiah (64:1ff.), the people who were restive under the rod of God's chastening, called on Him to do what He had done in earlier days: tear the heavens apart, make His name known again to His enemies, and be their redeemer (vv. 1-5). Despite the ceremonial uncleanness, moral depravity, and prayerlessness of the people generally, some of them called upon Him to remember, "We are the clay, you are the potter" (v. 8). They seemed to be appealing to the pride a worker takes in what he or she has made, a feeling that creates a bond between potter and pottery. Should not the divine potter have an analogous feeling for the nation He created at the time of the Exodus and had providentially shaped throughout its history? On that basis they prayed, "Do not be angry beyond measure, O Lord; do not remember our sins forever" (v. 9). That same bond formed the basis for prayers in other contexts (cf. Isa. 63:15-19; Jer. 14:9).

This attitude on the part of people who were being chastened for their sins sometimes spilled over into resentment and even questioning the very things God was doing in His control over history. Like opposition political parties who carp and complain about every act undertaken by the party in power, some Israelites constantly bellyached. They were sure that God was doing too little too late, that what He was doing would only make their lives more miserable, that He didn't have His priorities straight, and, finally, that He wasn't really competent to do the job.

We find such thoughts raised in Isaiah's writings:

> Why do you say, O Jacob,
>   and complain, O Israel,
> "My way is hidden from the Lord;
>   my cause is disregarded by my God?"
>
> (40:27)

> But Zion said, "The Lord has forsaken me,
>   the Lord has forgotten me."
>
> (49:14)

> . . . You forget the Lord your Maker, . . .
> that you live in constant terror every day.
>
> (51:13)

> "Declare to my people their rebellion . . .
> 'Why have we fasted,' they say,
>   'and you have not seen it?
> Why have we humbled ourselves,
>   and you have not noticed?'"
>
> (58:1, 3)

Some seemed to be quarreling with their Maker when He announced deliverance at the hand of Cyrus (45:9ff.). We can only conjecture who those might have been. Perhaps they were the ones who had come to terms with the exile, had settled down in Babylon, and were now prosperous in their new situations. To them a return from exile would be an irritating disruption in their affairs, a step down from prosperity (albeit in a foreign land) to a new life full of uncertainty and struggle.

In any case, Isaiah pronounced a "woe" on them. They were like mere pieces of pottery lying on the floor of the potter's workshop among other similar pieces. Some were asking the potter, "What are you making?" as if they had any say in the matter. Others were mocking the potter, saying that he had no hands and questioning his skill. The prophet likened all this to a baby's questioning his or her parents, "What have you brought to birth?" (v. 10). There might be some humor in these exchanges if the charges weren't so serious.

The Lord had a response. He reminded them of who He is—the Creator of heaven and earth with the right and the power to do what He pleases (vv. 11ff.). If He wished to bring about the restoration of Israel by means of a pagan ruler, sending some of His own people back to their own land, He would do so. And He would act "in my righteousness"; that is, when it was done no one would be able to quibble or resent what He had done.

The apostle Paul was clearly influenced by all these thoughts when discussing Israel's place in the economy of God (Rom. 9-11). The problem of God's righteousness was real. Romans 8 had closed with the promise of the security of the people of God: nothing "will be able to separate us from the love of God that is in Christ Jesus our Lord" (v. 39). But an objector might easily point to the Jewish nation at the time Paul was writing. Weren't *they* separated from His love? The epistle's next three chapters answer that question and a number of others related to it.

In his answer, Paul distinguished between believing and unbelieving Israel (9:6ff.). Because salvation is by grace, we may not look to an individual's life to explain why he or she is blessed (although we do look at the lives of sinners to understand why they are judged). God's sovereign election makes the difference:

"I will have mercy on whom I will have mercy, and I will have compassion on whom I will have compassion." (Exod. 33:19; Rom. 9:15)

Paul next considered another question. "Then why does God still blame us? For who resists his will?" Such a question might be asked simply as an explanation of this mystery, so far as it can be explained to us in our present state. But the question, as Paul considered it, was not a mere request for information. It was really talking back to God (v. 20).

We find a similar situation when we compare Zechariah's question ("How can I be sure of this?" in Luke 1:18) with Mary's inquiry ("How will this be?" in 1:34). In answer to the priest, Gabriel spoke sternly and pronounced a judgment for his unbelief. In his answer to the maiden, the angel explained some of the details of the virgin birth. God does not discourage our questions and often provides us with such answers as we are able to receive. But He resists those questions which reveal a hostile attitude and call into question His justice, wisdom, or love.

It is here that Paul invoked again the figure of the potter and the clay:

> "Shall what is formed say to him who formed it, 'Why did you make me like this?'" Does not the potter have the right to make out of the same lump of clay some pottery for noble purposes and some for common use? (vv. 20-21)

We may note how this quotation is a blend of the Old Testament passages studied above.

As we seek to understand "this high mystery," we must conclude that God is free to do His own will and that He does so in the full and free exercise of all of His attributes. (These attributes are not conflicting parts of God but rather descriptions of the ways He operates in human affairs.) Particularly, in the case of sinful humans who have by sin lost all their rights, He is free to show mercy and compassion to whom He wills without being obliged to justify His actions before unrepentant and rebellious human beings. The clay can never call the potter to the bar of its judgment.

This thought brings us back to the man of Gadara and his encounter with Jesus. There were many sinners in the region of the Gadarenes, many far more moral and caring than this poor wretch. What was it that could possibly commend him to Jesus? Just to ask that question is to answer it. Nevertheless, Jesus visited this man with salvation, while the others in their unbelief asked Him to leave. The Potter had worked in the clay to bring forth a beautiful piece of pottery for a noble purpose. The only hope for members of Adam's race is that the Potter will continue to do so—and we have the promise that He will!

Notes
[1] In an interesting shift in the metaphor, God used the verb for the potter's work to describe His shaping a disaster and devising a plan against the city.
[2] Dahood in *The Anchor Bible* gives this psalm a pre-exilic date.

22. *Shepherd*

Who can better tell us about the Shepherd than two men who had spent much of their lives with the sheep? Of the four places in Scripture where God is explicitly called "shepherd," three come to us from Jacob and David.

When he was dying and preparing to bless the sons of Joseph, Jacob looked back on almost a century and a half of life in Canaan, Haran, and Egypt. And he said,

> May the God before whom my fathers
> Abraham and Isaac walked,
> the God who has been my shepherd
> all my life to this day,
> the Angel who has delivered me from all harm
> —may he bless these boys.
>
> (Gen. 48:15-16)

Jacob had been a wandering sheep and had brought much grief upon himself. As he had said to Pharaoh some years before, "My years have been few and difficult" (47:9). But under the shepherding hand of God, Jacob had been delivered from lasting pain and loss, and now he was desiring that that same God would bless his grandsons.

Later, as he was blessing Joseph (49:24), Jacob said that

despite the hostility and attacks Rachel's son had endured during his lifetime,

> . . . his bow remained steady,
>   his strong arms remained limber,
>   because of the hand of the mighty one of Jacob,
>   because of the Shepherd, the Rock of Israel.

Joseph's personality was different from his father's. And his problems, from the human point of view, were largely the result of envy on his brothers' part. He needed a different kind of shepherding; namely, deliverance from those opposing him and support so that he might persevere through trouble and not take vengeance when given opportunity.

Reflecting on his life, which had been full of dramatic changes and constant dangers, David wrote the familiar words, "The Lord is my shepherd" (Ps. 23:1). He too had been surrounded by evils, most of them not of his own doing, and he too had been kept on a path of God's own appointment.

Asaph gives us the fourth instance of referring to God as a "shepherd" (Ps. 80):

> Hear us, O Shepherd of Israel,
>   you who lead Joseph like a flock. . . .
> Awaken your might;
>   come and save us.

> (vv. 1-2)

Like Jacob, the nation had brought most of its troubles on itself by straying from God (as we saw in the last chapter), and the psalmist's appeal for help was based on the shepherd-sheep relationship. Note how skillfully the writer used the vocabulary of a shepherd to describe the pitiful condition of the people:

> You have fed them with the bread of tears;
>   you *have made them drink* tears by the bowlful.
> (v. 5, emphasis added)

No wonder he prayed for better days.

From these biblical examples, we see two different objects of a shepherd's care. There are the straying sheep who need deliverance from the effects of their own wanderings (Jacob and the nation of Israel) and the powerless sheep who need protection from enemies who seek to kill them (Joseph and David).

To many of us, shepherding is not a familiar occupation. So it might be well to let Scripture provide us with some of the details of a shepherd's task:

- goes before, guides (Pss. 68:7; 77:20)
- leads to pasture, to water; feeds (Jer. 50:19)
- protects with rod and staff (Mic. 7:14)
- seeks lost sheep (Ezek. 34:11, 16)
- rescues when attacked (Ezek. 34:27ff.)
- gathers (Isa. 56:8)
- carries (Isa. 46:3f.).

Note that many of these actions are part of the picture in Psalm 23 and John 10. Taken together, this list of duties shows how complete and how constant is a shepherd's care for his flock. God as our shepherd cares no less fully and continuously for those who put their trust in Him.

Compare and contrast the lives of Joseph and David, both of whom suffered largely for righteousness' sake, with Jacob's struggles, mostly the result of his own misdeeds. We now see how God can properly be called our shepherd no matter what our lot in life may be. God saves all kinds of people, and, once saved, they are under His pastoral care.

God's Care for Jacob

Jacob's life was full of tension from the very beginning. When he and Esau jostled each other in Rebekah's womb, their action was interpreted symbolically: the twins would compete with each other, and the younger would win out (Gen. 25:22f.). As they were growing, Jacob alienated his brother by taking Esau's birthright (vv. 29ff.) and then stealing his blessing (27:1ff.). Esau's antipathy was so great that Jacob had to run for his life, spending 20 years in Haran with Laban and his family (27:41ff.).

In his dream at Bethel, Jacob heard God say, "I am with you and will watch over you" (28:15),[1] a promise he did not deserve and could hardly imagine to be true. He counted on God to "give me food to eat and clothes to wear" (v. 20), but God had far better things in store for him. He would be shepherd of every part of Jacob's life.

In Haran, Jacob was safe from Esau, but tension now developed between him and Laban for reasons ascribed to Laban alone. The older man's deception in forcing Jacob to marry Leah, the inevitable tension arising between two sisters married to the same man, the envy that grew in Laban's heart as he saw Jacob prospering and as his two daughters took Jacob's side against their father—when these occurred, "Jacob noticed that Laban's attitude toward him was not what it had been" (31:2).

The divine shepherd stepped in at this point and commanded Jacob to leave and return to Canaan (v. 3). The patriarch found himself between an angry brother whom he had robbed and an irate father-in-law whom he had deceived. When Laban pursued the fleeing caravan, wanting to recover his daughters, his cattle, and the stolen household gods, God intervened with a warning that prevented Laban from taking any hostile action (31:24). As Jacob was to have another confrontation with Esau, he was encouraged by the presence of God's angels (32:1). Then he made elaborate preparations to placate Esau but discovered they were unnecessary, for Esau's hatred had been mollified. So Jacob returned to his homeland wealthy and without the tensions that had haunted him for the past 20 years.

But now Jacob's life took a new turn as one occasion for grief followed another. First, Simeon and Levi reacted violently to the defilement of their sister, Dinah, and killed every male of Shechem, thus making it impossible for the new arrivals to stay in the city. Said Jacob, "You have brought trouble on me by making me a stench to the Canaanites and Perizzites" (34:30). Then Rebekah's nurse, a member of the family all of Jacob's life, died and was buried at Bethel (24:59; 35:8). Soon after, Rachel, his second but favorite wife, died in childbirth (48:7). While Jacob was mourning her death, Reuben had intercourse with Bilhah, Jacob's concubine and mother of some of his half-brothers (35:22f.). The full significance of this act is understood when we realize that Reuben, as firstborn, might have inherited Bilhah when his father died. From a cultural point of view, Reuben was acting as though his father were dead. He was dishonoring his parent in the eyes of the people of the city and thus adding the burden of shame to Jacob's already heavy heart. From a moral standpoint, this was an act of adultery. The incident was not forgotten, and Reuben lost his rights as the firstborn (Gen. 49:3f.; 1 Chron. 5:1f.). Isaac's death soon followed (35:29). Their father's burial brought Esau and Jacob together again, but no instance of tension or trouble remained between them.

For Jacob, the crushing blow came when he heard of the loss of Joseph from the brothers who sold him as a slave. Jacob knew nothing of Joseph's true affairs. As far as he was concerned, his favorite son was dead, and he carried that sorrow all his days until he met Joseph again in Egypt (42:38; 44:29, 31, 34).

Jacob did not have a happy life until God brought it to a triumphant end in Egypt. Contentment replaced the long-lasting sorrow. Somehow the heartaches of the past could be forgotten, because now he could see that the Shepherd had been with him all the way. Even when we have God as our shepherd, we are not guaranteed continual happiness and freedom from strain. But we do have the promise that He will be with us and that every event in our lives will have a meaning. As one of our favorite hymns, "How Firm a Foundation," puts it:

> When through the deep waters I call thee to go,
> The rivers of woe shall not thee overflow;
> For I will be with thee thy troubles to bless,
> And sanctify to thee thy deepest distress.
>
> When through fiery trials thy pathway shall lie,
> My grace all-sufficient, shall be thy supply;
> The flames shall not hurt thee; I only design
> Thy dross to consume, and thy gold to refine.
>
> E'en down to old age all my people shall prove
> My sovereign, eternal, unchangeable love;
> And when hoary hairs shall their temples adorn,
> Like lambs they shall still in my bosom be borne.

God's Care for Joseph

Joseph's sins are not portrayed in the Bible as are those of Jacob. Early on, Joseph alienated his brothers by giving a bad report about them, although we do not know what provoked it or what his motives were (37:2). He was certainly Jacob's favorite, and that did not sit well with ten older brothers. When they heard of his dreams, Joseph's brothers probably thought that he was God's favorite too. Joseph may have displayed some naivete in telling his parents and brothers what God had revealed about his future greatness, but there is no hint of pride in any of that (v. 5ff.).

Instead the Bible stresses much more God's purpose in Joseph's life. He had revealed to Abraham what would happen to the latter's descendants (15:7ff.)—how they would go to Egypt for four hundred years until Canaan was ready for judgment. Joseph was obviously God's instrument in the early stages of this plan, just as Pharaoh, Moses, and Aaron were to be used at its end. Joseph would precede his family to Egypt and establish a beachhead so that they would have a place there. The outworking of that plan is a supreme example of God's using the evil desires and actions of human beings for His own purposes (45:1-8; 50:19f.).

It should be stressed that though God used evil for good, that did not excuse the evils or make them good. The hatred and lies of the brothers, the lust and deceit of Potiphar's wife, the lapse of memory on the part of the chief butler—these are not examples for us to follow, and the Bible never puts them in a good light. But under the hand of the good Shepherd this one sheep, though wounded and dismayed by what certainly seemed undeserved bitterness and hostility, remained firm and steady in his determination to be true to God.

God does not have an *ad hoc* plan for our world. He does not revise it as history progresses. The things that occur are part of an all-wise counsel conceived from eternity, and all our lives fit part of that plan. That purpose is so much more important than our day-by-day experiences. Joseph's life was ordered so that God's plan would be fulfilled. Joseph understood this truth, and therein he found his comfort and fortitude.

God's Care for David

Like Joseph, David is another example of a righteous sufferer. True, Scriptures reveal more of his sins and of the decline in his power and prestige that came as a result of those sins. But for the most part, Scripture's emphasis is on David's piety (1 Kings 15:3-5) and on God's plan to use him to advance His kingdom on earth (2 Sam. 22:5-7).

The choice of David as Israel's king is another example of how sometimes God overturns human customs. Why should the youngest son of a Bethlehem shepherd ever be made king? That was certainly not Samuel's idea (1 Sam. 16:7) and probably not Jesse's (v. 11). What David's older brothers thought of it is not recorded. Eliab's jibe at the battle front (17:28) may be no more than that of an elder brother's disdain for the youngest, especially if the latter has caught him at a time of cowardice. In any case, David's brothers did not act toward him as Joseph's siblings had.

But Saul's reaction was another matter. In the rest of 1 Samuel (chaps. 18-31), two things were happening. The divine shepherd was protecting David from Saul and others as David wandered in the area surrounding the Dead Sea, and these experiences were being used to prepare him for reigning over the united kingdom. He would be a typical figure in the kingdom of God— the king par excellence of the Old Testament whose experiences would be recorded as prophetic of Jesus' own life and reign in the distant future. Those same experiences would give David opportunity to express his inner thought and faith in the psalms written during this period.

During this time God provided David with an odd set of helpers, as he fled from Saul's rage. This fact shows us the folly of trying to limit God's care to ordinary means. We are safe with Him even when we are not among our closest friends.

First, there was Saul's daughter Michal, who foiled an early attempt on his life (19:11). After that, God Himself sent a spirit of ecstasy among Saul and his men so that they were unable to carry out their plans to kill David (19:18ff.). Then, Saul's son Jonathan (20:1) became David's ally to alert him to Saul's schemes. In short order, David was fed by Philistines, Moabites, and Abigail as he made his escape from Saul. Only because he had a divine shepherd did David live to rule in Israel.

David was not marking time as he was awaiting God's time to ascend the throne. When the Shepherd is at work, He uses every moment to accomplish His purposes. David was learning how to trust God, how to command men, and how to deal with the Philistines, who were, for that time, the great enemy of the kingdom of God.

After Saul's death, David did become king over Judah for seven years and then was invited by Israel to rule the whole nation. But tension did not cease. He had to confront the hostility of Saul's rather large following, and his own supporters were not always wise in defending him (2 Sam. 2:8-4:12). Their attempts to defend him left David with a sad heart indeed. David desired to establish his kingdom on a solid religious base; he met with a sobering and stressful setback when he retrieved the ark not in accordance with the law. After Uzzah died, David went through a period of anger and anxious guilt (6:8ff.). Why did God condemn what he was doing when it was all for the good? The sheep was about to wander from full obedience to the Shepherd, and the rod and staff had to bring him back to reality.

Meanwhile, the king's army was busy conquering surrounding nations and making them vassals of the newly united kingdom. With some time now for reflection, David realized that the worship of the nation had fallen into disarray. There were two tabernacles, two high priests, and people were worshiping wherever they wished—all contrary to what Moses had said. David determined to rectify this and proclaimed he would build a house for God. His motive might have been commendable, but the Lord had other plans. God would build a house for David, a dynasty to rule over God's kingdom forever. And David would have a son who would build the temple. The lesson here is that even our plans flowing from proper motives may not be what God intends. The Shepherd must be sovereign, because only He knows the green pastures and the right paths.

The birth of that son was to be another example of God's

overruling sinful acts for good. Solomon, who was to build the temple and reign in David's place, was born amid the circumstances of David's adultery and murder. The legal penalty for either of those crimes was death, but through Nathan God granted David a full pardon. From the human standpoint, we may wonder what the people thought. Some unknown enemies of the Lord showed their contempt (12:14). Of course, monarchs would often sin with impunity, but David would feel the heavy hand of God's chastening in the months to come: "Out of your own household, I am going to bring calamity upon you" (v. 11). Bathsheba's child would die; Tamar would be disgraced; three of David's sons would be killed; Absalom would lead an insurrection, causing David to flee for his life. But all these calamities would be more than balanced by the promise: "The Lord has taken away your sin. You are not going to die" (v. 13).

Sometimes the Shepherd must be stern as He protects the sheep—a slight pain must be inflicted to prevent an even greater one. The slight pain was grievous indeed, but the sheep was still a member of the flock and continued to be under the Shepherd's care. Although outwardly David's reign seemed all downhill after these events, David's "last words" included the following:

> Is not my house right with God?
> 　Has he not made with me an everlasting covenant,
> 　arranged and secured in every part?
> Will he not bring to fruition my salvation
> 　and grant me my every desire?
>
> 　　　　　　　　　　　　　　　　(23:5)

David believed that goodness and love would follow him all the days of his life and that he would dwell in the house of the Lord forever. What more could a shepherd do for a sheep who was sorely tested and found wanting?

God's Care for His People

When the biblical writers looked back to the Exodus from Egypt and the desert journey Israel made on the way to Canaan, they sometimes spoke of these events under the figure of the shepherd and the sheep (Pss. 77:20; 78:52; Jer. 2:6). Similarly they looked upon their present conditions in the same light (Pss. 74:1; 80:1; 95:7; 100:3). When we visualize this relationship, we have an idyllic picture of sheep quietly grazing or following their shepherd as he leads them. The whole Old Testament becomes a record of God's shepherding individuals and peoples—feeding, leading, nursing, protecting them in their journey through life.

But when we recall the events recorded in Exodus and Numbers, it is difficult to fit into that pastoral scene the murmurings and rebellions that fill the pages of the books of Moses. This brings us to an important biblical perspective.

We may view the Bible's history *objectively* and stress God's work in fulfilling His will and blessing His people. From this point of view, Scripture speaks of compromising Lot as "a righteous man" (2 Pet. 2:7) and calls carping Israel "my Son" (Matt. 2:15). Another example of the objective side of Scripture is to see Christ in the Old Testament writings (Luke 24:25ff., 44). From this same standpoint we see God acting as shepherd in the corporate life of the nation, and from it we learn the lessons of His pastoral care. John Newton thus viewed the wilderness journey in the hymn "Glorious Things of Thee Are Spoken":

> Round each habitation hovering,
>   See the cloud and fire appear
> For a glory and a covering,
>   Showing that the Lord is near;
> Thus deriving from their banner
>   Light by night and shade by day,
> Safe they feed upon the manna
>   Which He gives them when they pray.

On the other hand, we may view those same events *subjectively*, that is, from the experiences of the people themselves. This is what Paul did in 1 Corinthians 10 and concluded that "God was not pleased with most of them" (v. 5). Individuals in the nation wandered from the Shepherd and were denied entrance into the Promised Land, but God saw to it that the nation would succeed.

In our Bible study we need a balance between these emphases. To stress the subjective side, ignoring entirely the objective, only leads to a human-centered view of Scripture. It reduces God to a helper at the beck and call of individuals in their need and misses the grand panorama of God's plan and purpose for the world. It is, unfortunately, the only way of interpreting Scripture that some people seem to know. Yet to overemphasize the objective side makes the Bible a recital of His words and mighty works but runs the danger of ignoring His work in individuals.

When we think of God as shepherd, we view His work objectively. He did lead the flock through the desert, and He does the same thing for His people today. When Jesus saw the people of Israel of His day far from God, they were like sheep without a shepherd (Matt. 9:36; 15:24). Some of them returned to the shepherd of their souls (1 Pet. 1:21). Those who would do so Jesus called His "little flock" and promised them the kingdom of God (Luke 12:32). After His triumphal ascension He was proclaimed to be "the great Shepherd of the sheep" (Heb. 13:20) and "the Chief Shepherd" of the flock (1 Pet. 5:4). The lesson to be drawn is that God's shepherding goes on. As He was with Jacob, Joseph, and David, as He did not forsake Israel even though Israel largely forsook Him, so He will be with His church and His saints today. To quote a hymn by Bernhardt Severin Ingemann:

Through the night of doubt and sorrow
    Onward goes the pilgrim band,
Singing songs of expectation,
    Marching to the promised land.
Clear before us through the darkness
    Gleams and burns the guiding light;
Brother clasps the hand of brother,
    Stepping fearless through the night. . . .

Onward, therefore, pilgrim brother,
    Onward, with the Cross our aid!
Bear its shame, and fight its battle,
    Till we rest beneath its shade!

Soon shall come the great awakening,
    Soon the rending of the tomb;
Then the scattering of all shadows,
    And the end of toil and gloom.

The picture of God our shepherd extends till the end of history, and even beyond. In the prophets He predicted a gathering of His scattered people (Isa. 40:10f.; Jer. 23:1ff.; 31:10; 50:19), and in heaven the shepherd figure persists. Concerning the multitude who had come out of great tribulation, one of the elders said to John:

they are before the throne of God
    and serve him day and night in his temple;
and he who sits on the throne will spread his tent over them.
Never again will they hunger;
    never again will they thirst.
The sun will not beat upon them,
    nor any scorching heat.
For the Lamb at the center of the throne will be their shepherd;
    he will lead them to springs of living water.
And God will wipe away every tear from their eyes.

                        (Rev. 7:15-17)

There are many mysteries regarding the afterlife, but we may confidently face them because the Lord is, and will be, our shepherd.

Notes

[1] Note how the phrase "God was [or "will be"] with them" is closely connected with His shepherding care:
- Jacob: Gen. 28:15, 20; 31:3, 5, 7, 42; 32:1, 9, 12; 33:11; 35:3; 46:3f.; 47:9; 48:21.
- Joseph: Gen. 39:2, 3, 21, 23; (Acts 7:9).
- David: 1 Sam. 15:18; 18:12, 14, 28; 23:14; 30:6; 2 Sam. 6:9.

A shepherd does not tend the flock from afar.

23. Refiner

David became very discouraged when he looked at the people of his day (Ps. 12). The godly were no more; the faithful had vanished. No one could be trusted, and no one's statements could be believed. Flattery and deception were the order of the day. Righteous people were terrified at the thought of what would happen if this situation were allowed to continue. How could they continue to do business with liars? How could government continue if public trust were completely undermined? The circumstances were similar to those of Psalm 11 where some people believed that the very foundations were being destroyed and that the only recourse for the righteous was to flee (vv. 1-3).

David had another idea. He prayed:

> May the Lord cut off all flattering lips
>   and every boasting tongue
> that says, "We will triumph with our tongues;
>   we own our lips—who is our master?"
>
> (Ps. 12:3-4)

God heard David's prayer and responded:

> "Because of the oppression of the weak
>   and the groaning of the needy,
> I will now arise," says the Lord.
>   "I will protect them from those who malign them."
>
> (v. 5)

Fine words, but words lose their value when liars and boasters abound. Then the psalmist remembered a very important truth:

> And the words of the Lord are flawless,
>> like silver refined in a furnace of clay,
>> purified seven times.
>
> (v. 6)

God would see to it that the words of the oppressors and liars would miserably fail. After all, they were only human words, uttered in defiance of God Himself; they would have no lasting value. These boastful utterances stand in direct contrast to God's words, which are like silver purified seven times in a furnace.

David was referring to a process well known in his time. There were different ways of refining ore, depending on the nature of the metal itself, but these all involved a furnace heated to a high temperature. The process also included the use of a crucible to hold the ore and some agent to help extract the metal. Also included were bellows to blow away the powdered impurities or ladles to skim off the molten slag, so that only the desired pure metal remained. The principal points of comparison in the figure are (1) the fire, which tests the ore and removes impurities, and (2) the products—the worthless slag, which can only be thrown away, and the refined metal, which is of high and lasting value or which has a greater efficiency and durability as a result of its passing through the fire.

An End Product of Refining

David was speaking of God's Word in the highest terms. To refine silver seven times is to remove all the dross, so that what remains is pure, valuable, and trustworthy. God's Word is like such highly refined silver. It comes to us tested and tried because it is grounded on God's omniscience. It alone is flawless and can be completely trusted. David, who was so concerned about the moral conditions of his day, had at least one trustworthy recourse—God's Word was true. And when God said He would arise and protect the righteous from those maligning them, His Word would certainly come to pass.

Similar statements are to be found in Scripture (2 Sam. 22:31; Pss. 18:30; 119:40; Prov. 30:5). The emphasis in all these verses is not on the process of taking out impurities, as if the Bible once written required editing to correct its statements. These verses stress that the Bible is like the finished product, and there are no impurities present because the character of God stands behind His words. Here one may find stability and security amid the lies and false statements of one's neighbors.

This is an important truth for our day, because we are being tempted to believe there are better ways of coping with life than the ways revealed in the Bible. After we had studied some passages on church discipline, a man once said to me, "Now let's get back to the real world where we have to deal with real people." Somehow he felt that the Bible was too idealistic, and for that reason it hadn't worked in actual human experience. In truth, the church in the past has failed in some instances of its disciplining, but today it fails even more in hardly disciplining at all! God says that His Word has been tested and it is trustworthy, certainly more trustworthy than the changing attitudes of modern society.

Testing for Precious Metals

The Bible also presents a vivid picture of God as refiner of His people, and here the emphasis is on the process of refining itself. One of the clearest examples is found in Proverbs 17:3:

> The crucible for silver and the furnace for gold,
>   but the Lord tests the heart.

A refiner may have different purposes in mind. He may be looking for gold or silver in the raw ore set before him. This process we call "testing." Or he may wish to purify the precious metal already identified. This is known as "refining" per se.

In Proverbs 17:3 the stress is on the former. A refiner looks at the crude ore before him and wonders whether there is anything worthwhile in it. So he subjects a specimen of it to the refining process to get his answer. God as refiner also knows that since the time of Adam, sin must be taken into account in His dealings with us. Because our "heart is deceitful above all things and beyond cure" (Jer. 17:9), our faith must be shown to be true faith, and the refining process is God's way of determining it. Ezekiel describes the refining going on in his day. Lamentably it resulted in the finding that Israel was dross:

> Son of man, the house of Israel has become dross to me; all of them are the copper, tin, iron and lead left inside a furnace. They are but the dross of silver. Therefore this is what the Sovereign Lord says: "Because you have all become dross, I will gather you into Jerusalem. As men gather silver, copper, iron, lead and tin into a furnace to melt it with a fiery blast, so will I gather you in my anger and my wrath and put you inside the city and melt you. I will gather you and I will blow on you with my fiery wrath, and you will be melted inside her. As silver is melted in a furnace, so you will be melted inside her, and you will know that I the Lord have poured out my wrath upon you." (22:18-22)

But there are happier results of God's testing. The Macedonian churches had been tried by poverty and affliction, and they had passed the test brilliantly. "Out of the most severe trial, their overflowing joy and their extreme poverty welled up in rich generosity" (2 Cor. 8:1ff.). They showed the grace of giving Paul sought for in all his converts, especially those at Corinth.

Testing is a very important and, unless it becomes morbid introspection, a very wholesome part of Christian growth. We should remember the parable of the sower (not all the seeds produced good fruit) and the warnings found in 1 Corinthians 10 and in Hebrews as well as the words of Jesus, "Not everyone who says to me, 'Lord, Lord,' will enter the kingdom of heaven, but only he who does the will of my Father who is in heaven." Then we can appreciate how essential is Paul's warning, "Examine yourselves to see whether you are in the faith" (2 Cor. 13:5). There will not be much growth in the Christian life until the individual determines whether he or she is "in the faith."

We determine this matter by assessing the way we react and respond to the disciplines of life. If we are truly Christians, we will "be exercised" by our experiences (cf. Heb. 12:11, KJV), responding to them in faith in God's promises. When we discover that our reactions are those of unbelief and bitterness, we then learn that we are not in the faith. The testings at Kadesh-Barnea showed the basic difference between two groups of spies. The two faithful spies responded to the challenge of Canaan by urging obedience to God despite the obstacles of fortified cities and high walls; the ten timid spies became fearful, prompted by their lack of confidence in God and His promises and the seeming enormity of the task of taking the land. Because of this test, only Caleb and Joshua were allowed to enter Canaan. The others "were not able to enter, because of their unbelief" (Heb. 3:18).

Refining the Crude Ore

The ore as it comes from the ground and the Christian who has been saved from sin—both must be refined. The reason for this is not hard to find. Even though we may be justified by faith, our sin still offends a holy God, and it must be purged before we can stand in His presence. Just as silver is useless until the dross is removed, so evil must go before there can be true righteousness (Prov. 25:4f.). Much of the dross of sin is removed by the trials and tests that come to us.

Peter was persuaded of the good spiritual health of his readers. They had received the new birth; they had been introduced to a living hope and an imperishable inheritance; they were being shielded by God's power and could therefore rejoice greatly (1 Pet. 1:3ff.).

But a refining process was indicated for them. "For a little while" they would have "all kinds of trials." Their joy would not be taken from them, but they would know grief in the midst of joy. These trials came for two reasons: (1) their faith would be proved genuine and (2) this same faith would produce a character that would bring glory at Christ's coming. A study of

Scripture will reveal that this refining process is God's program for His people throughout their history.

Testing and Refining During the Exodus

The Exodus was one of the great moments in the history of refining the people of God. In the wilderness the nation was forced to depend wholly on God and to forget the ways it had learned in Egypt. For this reason the whole experience is called "an iron-smelting furnace" (Deut. 4:20; 1 Kings 8:51; Jer. 11:4).

Don't ever underestimate the trauma the Israelites endured. First, there was the long period of slavery, an experience purposefully degrading and dehumanizing. Then came a glimmer of hope when Moses and Aaron arrived on the scene with word that God would deliver them. But their expectations were soon dashed when the Egyptians turned a deaf ear to Moses' pleas. Then came the two plagues when all the people found frogs in their beds, ovens, and kneading troughs (Exod. 8:3) and gnats on themselves and their animals (v. 18). The other plagues were not directed at the Israelites, but even in this they learned how they depended on God's will for their very existence, a truth they would live with in the desert for the rest of their lives. Even after the Israelites had put blood on their door frames, their faith was once more put to the test as they waited for the plague to pass over their houses. Next came the trial at Pi Hahiroth, where God permitted them to be completely hemmed in by the sea before and the Egyptian armies behind. Their faith faltered (Exod. 14:10ff.) but was vindicated when the Lord brought deliverance. "And when the Israelites saw the great power of the Lord displayed against the Egyptians, the people feared the Lord and put their trust in him and in Moses his servant" (v. 31).

The whole ordeal had lasted many weeks (or months), and the people were kept on "pins and needles" for all that time. They wondered whether the God who had allowed them to suffer under the Egyptians for so long would eventually rescue them. This period surely was "an iron-smelting furnace."

For most of that generation, the lessons of the Exodus were

completely lost. The people could not receive the message; it "was of no value to them, because those who heard did not combine it with faith" (Heb. 4:2). They had never accepted God's way as theirs and so were found to be dross. But the writer of Hebrews counsels us to learn what they could not: let us "not fall by following their example of disobedience" (v. 11).

Testing and Refining During the Period of Judges

During the time of the judges people were doing what was right in their own eyes. There was little revelation from God, and it would have been easy for Gideon to take all the credit for his victory over the Midianites. To prevent such a problem, God reduced the size of Gideon's army to such small proportions that the people would have to believe that only He had brought the victory. The Midianites appeared "like swarms of locusts" (Judg. 6:5; 7:12) (even after 120,000 of their swordsmen had fallen before Gideon, 15,000 were still left to fight). Against such a huge army, only 32,000 came to the support of Gideon, but God said they were too many. After 22,000 fearful men returned home, the 10,000 remaining seemed few indeed against the horde of Midian. Still, God called for more reductions in troop strength. So 300 were separated from the others who were otherwise willing to fight. The process was called "sifting" (7:4; in other contexts this Hebrew word is translated "refine"). "Three hundred men lapped with their hands to their mouths. All the rest got down on their knees to drink" (v. 6). Although the Bible does not say so, some commentators think that their postures in drinking revealed an attitude of readiness, or the lack of it, for battle and that God chose whose who were ready. In any case, the army was now reduced to the point where confidence had to be wholly in the Lord. There was no room for human boasting.

Testing and Refining During the Exile

The prophets viewed the coming exile as another refining experience in the life of the people. God told Jeremiah that He had no alternative but to bring judgment (9:7). He explained through Isaiah that He would do this for His own sake; for by the covenant He was so identified with them that He was being defamed by their wickedness and His glory given to idols (48:10f.). Sanctification (the purpose of refining) has its human side. We are being made holy because that is our true destiny, and therefore it is for our good. But there is also the divine side. We represent God in the world and act as His agents. People then hold God responsible for our actions. When those actions present a false picture of Him, He must step in and remover the slag of sin and unrighteousness.

Judah had become so like the idolatrous nations that one could not tell the one from the other. Just as the pagans had no thought for God, Judah had no time for Him either. Such dross had to be removed. Only this can explain the savagery God permitted of the Babylonians. The exile began in siege and famine. These events were followed by bloodshed and destruction (cf. 2 Kings 24; Jer. 52; Lam. gives many details). Finally, the Babylonians deported the few who were left. With none of their possessions except what might be carried as they trudged to Babylon, the exiles had lost everything they cherished. In the exile, they learned that these things were not what counted in life; what counted was God's presence with them (Ezek. 11:16; cf. Exod. 33:15). Some of them returned to put the lessons into practice. They would rebuild the temple and the city with the help of God, not with the assistance of surrounding peoples. Zerubbabel, Ezra and Nehemiah, Haggai, Zechariah and Malachi represent the purged remnant. Alas, once again the faithful ones seemed to be a minority, even among those who had been in exile.

Testing and Refining Today

Those same prophets spoke of a time of testing and purifying to come when God's people would be restored to living fellowship with him (Dan. 11:35; 12:10; Zech. 13:9). This would occur in the days of Messiah. In Malachi's day, mockers were saying,

> "All who do evil are good in the eyes of the Lord and he is pleased with them" or "Where is the God of justice?" (2:17)

God's reply to the scoffers was to announce the coming of His messenger who would prepare the way for Him, and then He ("the Lord you are seeking," "the messenger of the covenant, whom you desire") would appear. Clearly, this refers to Messiah and to His predecessor, John the Baptist. It would be a frightening time:

> But who can endure the day of his coming? Who can stand when he appears?" (3:2)

The reason for such fear? "He will be like a refiner's fire. . . . he will purify the Levites and refine them like gold and silver" (v. 3). Although we would not want to press the numbers, Malachi was talking of very high temperatures. The melting points are about 1800° F for silver and 1945° F for gold. The fire is hot indeed, and the process of refining can therefore be very painful.

The Levites and priests had come in for great rebuke in the early chapters of Malachi. Showing contempt for God's name, they had defiled His altar (1:6f.). They did not set their hearts to honor Him, but had turned from the way of God and had caused many others to stumble by their false teaching and bad example. They had violated the covenant with Levi (2:2ff.). As spiritual leaders, their refining was most necessary if the people were to return to the Lord.

But the people themselves were to be rebuked. Included among the remnant, once "purified" by the exile, were now sorcerers, adulterers, and perjurers. There were those who defrauded laborers, oppressed widows and orphans, and deprived aliens of justice. In doing these wicked things the people did not fear God.

A refining process was indicated so that the Lord

> will have men who will bring offerings in righteousness, and the offerings of Judah and Jerusalem will be acceptable to the Lord as in days gone by. (Mal. 3:3-4)

Note the total reversal that took place in the priests' actions. Where once they had offered defiled food and diseased animals (1:7-8), they now brought offerings in righteousness. Such a thing could only happen when the Refiner had done His work—separating the dross and purifying the remaining gold and silver, a process that must go on until the Lord returns.[1] One significant example of this was recorded by Luke: "a large number of priests became obedient to the faith" (Acts 6:7).

Some Lessons

These Old Testament experiences were written to teach us the continuous need for a refining process in our lives and in the life of the church (Rom. 15:4; 1 Cor. 10:6, 11). There are three important lessons to be learned.

First, *testing* finds what is genuine. This is a standard operating procedure in the believer's life:

> I know, my God, that you test the heart and are pleased with integrity. (1 Chron. 29:17)

David wrote in the present tense, an indication that God was doing this all the time. Jeremiah knew the same truth, and he had the confidence to believe that he would pass the test while his contemporaries would not (12:3; 20:12).

Second, *refining* removes the dross. This is another normal experience in the Christian life. James tells us to accept refining joyfully since we know that it will, in the end, do us good and we will be mature (1:2ff.). This truth comforted Job somewhat when his friends failed him (23:10), and we meet a renewed Job in the denouement of the story (chap. 42).

Third, we should *pray* that God will bring such testing and purifying into our lives. Armed with the truth of this principle, David was prompted to pray for further testing because he understood the necessity for removing offensive ways from his life (Ps. 139:23f.).

Robert Browning put into the mouth of his Rabbi Ben Ezra a modern expression of what the biblical saints were expressing:

> Then, welcome each rebuff
> That turns earth's smoothness rough,
> Each stings that bids nor sit nor stand but go!
> Be our joys three-parts pain!
> Strive, and hold cheap the strain;
> Learn, nor account the pang; dare, never grudge the throe!
>
> For thence,—a paradox
> Which comforts while it mocks,—
> Shall life succeed in that it seems to fail:
> What I aspired to be,
> And was not, comforts me:
> A brute I might have been, but would not sink i' the scale.

Notes
[1] Hengstenberg, in his *Christology of the Old Testament* (p. 603), suggests that the Hebrew verb for "he will sit" (v. 3) may be understood to refer to a long-term operation.

24. Lord and Master

When we hear the word *master* today, we often think of a teacher in a private school or a winner of a golf tournament in Georgia. When we think of *lord*, we are apt to think of people in Europe whose ancestors once had power and money but who now must rent their estates as museums to make ends meet.

The word *Lord* as a religious expression is used, and abused, in much of our speech today. Just because someone uses the word often does not mean he or she is a pious person. In fact, that person could be blaspheming. Jesus was troubled by the attitude of His hearers early in His ministry. He asked, "Why do you call me, 'Lord, Lord,' and do not do what I say?" (Luke 6:46). There is obviously an empty and, therefore, blasphemous use of the word. Its proper use is accompanied by the worship and obedience due the Lord. To quote Jesus again:

> Not everyone who says to me, "Lord, Lord," will enter the kingdom of heaven, but only he who does the will of my Father who is in heaven. Many will say to me on that day, "Lord, Lord, did we not prophesy in your name, and in your name drive out demons and perform many miracles?" Then I will tell them plainly, "I never knew you. Away from me, you evildoers!" (Matt. 7:21-23)

If we are to embrace the scriptural meanings of the words, *lord* and *master*, we must see how they were understood at the time they were spoken.

Authority and Power

In both testaments the words in the original languages may signify the respect one person has for another, much as we use the term *sir* (Gen. 18:12 and 1 Pet. 3:6; Acts 16:30). Often a lord is recognized as having great authority, and so he is shown reverence and fear. For example, Joseph properly received that title when Pharaoh elevated him to the post of chief administrator in his land:

> He made him master [lord] of his household,
>   ruler over all he possessed.
>
> > (Ps. 105:21)

When Joseph's brothers came to buy grain in Egypt because of a famine in Canaan, they met with the chief administrator. Though they did not recognize him as Joseph, the brothers understood that this man was a high official in the government. They "bowed down to him with their faces to the ground" (Gen. 42:6) and called him "lord" (vv. 10, 30, 33; many vv. in chap. 44). Partly because of Joseph's position and partly because of the guilt they felt, the brothers called themselves his slaves (50:18). "Lord" for them was an awesome title, as this official had the power of life and death.

When the centurion met Jesus in Capernaum, he called Him "Lord" (Matt. 8:5ff.). This might be translated as "sir," but later on it is clear that he was showing Jesus far more than mere respect. He asked Jesus to heal a valued servant, who had a painful terminal disease. When Jesus agreed to visit the man and perform the healing, the soldier objected, for he did not feel worthy to receive Christ into his home. He went on to say that, as a soldier somewhere in the middle of the chain of command, he could speak to a subordinate and expect obedience. He was implying that Jesus as Lord could do much more than that because He was a greater person than the centurion. A Galilean Jew greater than a Roman soldier? Jesus was astonished at this great faith—a faith He had not found among the Israelites. That kind of faith would admit even Gentiles to the messianic feast, along with such giants as Abraham, Isaac, and Jacob. But to the centurion's childlike faith, it was all very simple. The Lord could say a word, and a miracle would happen. Lordship implied awesome power and authority.

Ownership

In Jesus' parables *lord* takes on an added meaning. In the parable of the workers in the vineyard (Matt. 20:1ff.), the landowner is called "lord" (v. 8, KJV). As lord, he has the right to do what he wants with his money. When Jesus applied the parable to the kingdom, He asserted His right to reward those in the kingdom according to His own standards: "So the last will be first, and the first will be last" (v. 16). Here was an authority of the most radical kind, one that did not have to conform to accepted standards and laws.

In the parable of the tenants (Matt. 21:33ff.), the lord (v. 40, KJV) enforced his proper right to collect the fruits of the land. He punished the rebellious tenants and replaced them with those "who will give him his share of the crop at harvest time" (v. 41). Here the authority was long-suffering, but in the end it was irresistible and complete (v. 44).

In Luke 12, Jesus told His disciples not to be afraid of anyone who might persecute them and destroy their bodies, but He did warn them to fear God "who, after the killing of the body, has power to throw you into hell" (v. 5). He followed this warning with a series of exhortations regarding the final judgment. In the parable of the faithful and wise manager (vv. 42ff.), a master gave his steward and servants under him commands regarding their duties while he was away. Upon his return, the master dealt out rewards and punishments according to their faithfulness. And the punishment fit the crime. The servants who understood what was expected of them and disobeyed suffered greatly. Those who disobeyed but were ignorant received leniency. Here accountability is an essential element in our understanding of a lord-servant relationship.

In these parables Jesus was using the word "lord" to convey the thought of an authority that, while not whimsical and arbitrary, did not brook any opposition and was conscious of rights and privileges belonging solely to the owner of property. This view is consistent with the Old Testament picture of God as Lord. When the psalmist saw nations and peoples rebelling against the Lord and His Messiah, he warned them of how hopeless it would be:

> The One enthroned in heaven laughs;
>   the Lord scoffs at them.
>
> (Ps. 2:4)

The distance between the Lord of all the earth and the mightiest of earth's armies makes even their foremost efforts at independence a joking matter.

Protection

There is also a human side to lordship. Faithful servants may expect protection from their powerful masters. The Psalms include a number of instances where the writers face great danger because of enemies, and so they call upon their Lord for the protection promised in their covenant relationship. In Psalm 71, the writer was oppressed by evil and cruel men (v. 4). Evidently along in years (vv. 9, 18), he had experienced God's deliverances before (vv. 5f., 17). His enemies were planning to take him by force, being persuaded that God had forsaken him (vv. 10f.). But the psalmist found comfort at the thought that he had a sovereign Lord. The powerful Lord came to his rescue, clothed in righteousness and faithfulness (vv. 19, 22, 24), and put the enemies to shame and confusion.

In Psalm 140 David's enemies were men of violence, prepared to meet him both in the marketplace and on field of battle. In either case, the sovereign Lord would hear his cry for mercy and not let their plans succeed.

In Psalm 109 David spoke of a similar situation. The danger here seemed not to be from physical force but from lies and slander (v. 2), even from those who had been his friends (vv. 4f.). David called upon his sovereign Lord (v. 21) and prayed for deliverance "out of the goodness of your love" (v. 21). Although he had been reduced to a poor spirit and a weak body, David's confidence in God remained unshaken:

> For he stands at the right hand of the needy one,
> to save his life from those who condemn him.
> (v. 31)

In Psalm 141 the thought of the sovereign Lord kept the writer from the snares and traps laid by his detractors (v. 9); it also kept him from falling into evil as he opposed them. He wanted his prayer to be as pure and acceptable as the burnt offering and incense offered each evening in the temple. The offering was to be ceremonially clean and holy with an aroma pleasing to the Lord (Lev. 1); the incense was to be "salted and pure and sacred" (Exod. 30:35). The psalmist might have been tempted to join with evildoers or to use their own tactics in retaliation against them. But his eyes were fixed on the sovereign Lord, and he had the confidence that he would pass by them in safety (vv. 8ff.). Thus a real sanctifying effect took place in his life. To have such a Master is to know true holiness.

Each of these aspects of lordship—authority and power, ownership, and protection—is amply illustrated in the life of the apostle Paul.

Saul's Conversion

Saul, a blasphemer, a persecutor, and a violent man, heard Jesus say, "Saul, Saul, why do you persecute me?" Lying prostrate in the roadway, Saul asked, "Who are you, Lord?"[1] (Acts 9:4f.). He had recognized the Lord before he knew that He was Jesus. He thought he had been serving the Lord all his life, and during that time he certainly did not believe that Jesus was the

Lord. Yet this realization made all the difference in the new apostle's life.

Whenever Paul's apostleship was called into question (as it was in Jerusalem, Corinth, and Galatia), he referred his critics to the moment of his conversion (Acts 26:14; 1 Cor. 9:1; 15:8; 2 Cor. 4:6; Gal. 1:16). This experience caused the sudden change which took place in his life, and it explained why he no longer "kicked against the goads" of God's sovereignty. It also gave him credentials equal to those of Peter and the other apostles, so that whenever a difference of opinion arose, his word was received on a par with theirs.

But beyond those things, his conversion experience provided Paul with a revelation that became the heart of his lifelong message. God, whom Paul thought he was serving as he persecuted the followers of Jesus, showed him that Jesus was His Son. Paul reasoned that if Jesus was God's Son, then He was the Lord of glory. The apostle confessed that he was able to do thus only because the Holy Spirit had empowered him (1 Cor. 12:3).

As Paul understood the word, *lordship* entailed all these ideas and much more. As Lord, God is free to do all His holy will and to command others to do it, too. We must be reminded frequently that the Bible does not offer advice, but it is full of commands. Although it is not always wise to do so, advice may be ignored without penalty. But commandments always bring with them a penalty when they are disobeyed or ignored.

Some years ago a weekly news magazine carried a story of a clergyman from Europe who visited the United States. He had come not to speak in, but to listen to, the churches of America. After he had completed his visit and was embarking on a ship to return home, he was asked to summarize the many sermons he had heard. He paused and then said, "My brothers, I urge you to do better." If this was an accurate representation of our condition in those days, no wonder we are in the mess we are! Didn't anyone preach, "Thus says the Lord"?

Paul recognized that Jesus is Lord, and his life was changed. Some measure of the dramatic change that lordship made in Paul's life can be seen in the reversals he experienced after his conversion:

Before Paul Met Jesus	After Paul Met Jesus
•approved Stephen's death (Acts 7:60)	•could wish he were cursed (Rom. 9:3)
•persecuted house to house (8:3)	•witnessed house to house (Acts 20:20)
•dragged people to prison (8:3)	•imprisoned often (2 Cor. 11:23)
•wanted to take them bound to Jerusalem (9:2)	•went to Jerusalem bound in the Spirit (Acts 20:22)
•did everything possible to oppose Jesus (26:9)	•was eager to preach (Rom. 1:15)
•forced others to blaspheme (26:11)	•led Gentiles to obey (Rom. 15:18)
•traveled to foreign cities to persecute (26:11)	•preached where Christ was not known (Rom. 15:20)
•persecuted intensely (Gal. 1:13)	•was flogged severely (2 Cor. 11:23)

It is clear that Paul's conversion brought no lessening in the intensity of his efforts and no curtailing of his activities. But there came a new *direction* for these abilities and efforts, produced by the revelation and subsequent conviction that Jesus is Lord.

Obedience and Faith

To confess that Jesus is Lord is a step of faith, and to act on that confession requires even more faith because God's lordship brings both uncertainty and certainty into the lives of believers. Consider how Paul's obedience to the will of God made much of his life uncertain:

- the amount of his salary and how often he received it (Phil. 4:15ff.)
- where he would go next and how he would get there (Acts 16:6f.; 1 Thess. 2:18) (note the activities of both the Spirit and Satan affecting Paul's journeys)
- the kind and intensity of his next persecution (2 Cor. 11:22ff.)
- who would desert him next (2 Tim. 4:10, 16)
- when and how he would die (Phil. 1:22f.)

Clearly, only faith in a sovereign Lord could support Paul in such circumstances; yet it was that very lordship which produced these conditions. A man like Paul who did not have Jesus as Lord might have had an easy and comfortable life, but no one can accuse Paul of that!

Yet God's sovereignty over Paul made some things certain, beyond any reasonable doubt. Consider these claims of Paul:

- his needs would always be supplied (Phil. 4:19)
- he would have strength for each day's labors (Phil. 4:12)
- every event of his life would be so controlled that in the end it would be pronounced "good" (Rom. 8:28)
- he had a treasure in heaven that could never be taken from him (2 Tim. 1:12; 4:7f.)

To be a servant of the living God brings great advantages indeed.

It was essential that Paul be given these assurances from the start. His life was in constant opposition to enemies of the Gospel—some willful, some ignorant. He had to stand up to his former associates, the Jews who would have killed them if they could. He had to oppose those within the church who would pervert the message by adding to it unnecessary observance of Jewish ceremonies (as in Galatia) or worship of angels (as in Colosse). Paul had to go his lonely way to evangelize the Gentiles and then had to protect them from being treated as second-class citizens when they believed. He had to defend himself against heathen who would treat him as a god—or kill him! And, of course, behind all these human enemies stood Satan and his demons. Only the conviction of God's lordship kept Paul obedient to his heavenly calling.

Lordship Humbles

The thought of lordship humbles every one of God's servants to the point where he or she feels unworthy of the least of His mercies. Such a one is dismayed at the great lack of commitment on the part of Christians. Jesus commended the devotion of John the Baptist (Matt. 11:7ff.), but John did not feel worthy even of the menial task of loosing and removing Jesus' sandals (3:11). Despite all the grace exhibited in Paul's ministry, he still considered himself the worst of sinners (1 Tim. 1:15f.). Note that Paul was speaking of his *present* condition ("I am"), not just his preconversion conduct. After some years of ministry, he was still "the least of God's people" (Eph. 3:8).[2]

Lordship Exalts

At the same time, lordship ennobles God's servants. What a glorious privilege to be numbered among the servants of the Lord of Lords! That privilege was Paul's from the very moment of his conversion, and it belongs to every one of the saints. Paul prayed that the Ephesians might understand their exalted position that resulted from their union with the resurrected Christ. God

> seated him at his right hand in the heavenly realms, far above all rule and authority, power and dominion, and every title that can be given.... And God placed all things under his feet and appointed him to be head over everything for the church. (1:20-22)

Consider His exalted place in the universe, remembering that we belong to Him and He to us. See what exaltation is ours, for we too live in heavenly places. His lordship guarantees all our blessings and privileges. He is ruling over all things for the sake of the church, and, as we represent Him on earth, we are under His jurisdiction and protection.

I remember years ago hearing a former Marine telling of his experiences while stationed at various diplomatic residences in Washington, D.C. He knew some of the personnel quite well and became acquainted with their lifestyles and attitudes. Something significant happened to them, however, when they were called upon to make appearances at the White House or State Department on behalf of their governments. They dressed in their finest, walked with unusual dignity, and delivered their government's message with precision and eloquence. The

Marine said that the diplomats became different people when acting in behalf of their sovereigns. How much greater dignity and honor attaches to the ambassadors of Christ when we act and speak in His name!

A wonderful simplicity can come into our lives when we recognize Jesus as Lord. As Frederick Faber said in his familiar hymn "There's a Wideness in God's Mercy,"

> If our love were but more simple,
>> We should take Him at His word;
> And our lives would be all sunshine
>> In the sweetness of our Lord.

The point is often made that once Christ's sovereignty is recognized and a Christian's life is based on it, many decisions will already have been made. When we wholeheartedly obey the form of teaching to which we were entrusted (Rom. 6:17), we will already have said yes to God's commands because like the centurion we know what it is to be under authority. And we will have obeyed His precepts because we want to please our commanding officer (2 Tim. 2:4). We may avoid much of the agony of decision making by realizing that when we became Christians, we implicitly made many of those decisions in advance. We need only to ratify them once again. Clearly our recognition of God's sovereignty brings with it peace and stability.

Notes
[1] We may not know precisely what the word "Lord" meant to Saul when he used it on the Damascus road. Clearly he was not calling Jesus "sir," although the word is sometimes used that way in Greek. It is probable that under the illumination of the Spirit, Paul was acknowledging Jesus as God and the master of the life he was just beginning to live. The lordship of Christ became the dominant theme of Paul's preaching and writing ministry.

[2] As synonyms of "least" Arndt and Gingrich give "quite unimportant, insignificant" (*A Greek-English Lexicon of the New Testament*, 248).

References

Andersen, Francis I. and David Noel Freedman. *The Anchor Bible: Hosea.* Garden City, New York: Doubleday, 1980.

Arndt, William F. and F. Wilbur Gingrich. *A Greek-English Lexicon of the New Testament.* Chicago: University of Chicago, 1957.

Barker, Kenneth, ed. *The NIV Study Bible.* Grand Rapids: Zondervan, 1985.

Botterweck, G. J. and H. Ringgren, eds. *Theological Dictionary of the Old Testament.* Grand Rapids: Eerdmans, 1974.

Browning, Robert. *The Poems and Plays of Robert Browning.* New York: Modern Library, 1934.

Calvin, John. *Commentaries on the Twelve Minor Prophets.* Grand Rapids: Baker, 1979.

――――. *Commentary on the Book of Psalms.* Edinburgh: Calvin Translation Society, 1845.

――――. *Institutes of the Christian Religion.* Edited by John T. McNeill. 2 vols. Philadelphia: Westminster, 1960.

The Confession of Faith Agreed upon by the Assembly of Divines at Westminster. Glasgow: Free Presbyterian Publications, 1973.

Dahood, Mitchell. *The Anchor Bible: Psalms.* Garden City, New York: Doubleday, 1965.

Ellison, H. L. *Ezekiel: The Man and His Message.* Grand Rapids: Eerdmans, 1956.

223

Geisler, Norman L., ed. *Inerrancy.* Grand Rapids: Zondervan, 1979.

Geldenhuys, Norval. *Commentary on the Gospel of Luke.* NICNT. Grand Rapids: Eerdmans, 1951.

Gleick, James. "Using Chaos to Make Order." *Smithsonian* 18, no. 9 (1987):122-34.

Gore, Rick. "Extinctions." *National Geographic* 175, no. 6 (June 1989):662-99.

Guthrie, D. and J. A. Motyer, eds. *The New Bible Commentary: Revised.* Grand Rapids: Eerdmans, 1970.

Hendriksen, William. *New Testament Commentary: Romans; Galatians and Ephesians; Thessalonians, Timothy and Titus.* Grand Rapids: Baker, 1981, 1981, 1979.

Hengstenberg, E. W. *Christology of the Old Testament.* Grand Rapids: Kregel, 1970.

Henry, Matthew. *A Commentary on the Whole Bible.* Old Tappan, N. J.: Revell Co., n.d.

Keil, C. F., and F. Delitzsch. *Biblical Commentary on the Old Testament: The Books of Samuel* (1950); *The Books of Kings* (1965); *Proverbs of Solomon* (n.d.); *The Prophecies of Isaiah* (1969); *The Twelve Minor Prophets* (1951). Grand Rapids: Eerdmans.

Konig, Adrio. *Here Am I!* Grand Rapids: Eerdmans, 1982.

Lakoff, G., and M. Johnson. *Metaphors We Live By.* Chicago: University of Chicago, 1980.

Oswalt, John N. *The Book of Isaiah, Chapters 1-39.* NICOT. Grand Rapids: Eerdmans, 1986.

Owen, John. *The Works of John Owen.* Edited by William H. Goold. London and Edinburgh: Johnstone and Hunter, 1851.

Oxford English Dictionary. Compact Edition. Oxford: Oxford University Press, 1971.

Pratt, Richard L. *Pray with Your Eyes Open.* Phillipsburg, N.J.: Presbyterian and Reformed, 1988.

Ridderbos, Herman. *The Coming of the Kingdom.* Philadelphia: Presbyterian and Reformed, 1962.

Swete, Henry B. *The Apocalypse of St. John.* Grand Rapids: Eerdmans, n.d.

Tenney, Merrill C. *The Zondervan Pictorial Encyclopedia of the Bible*. Grand Rapids: Zondervan, 1975.

Trinity Hymnal. Philadelphia: Great Commission, 1961.

Twain, Mark. *The Adventures of Tom Sawyer*. New York: Grossett and Dunlap, 1922.

Westcott, Brooke Foss. *The Epistles of St. John*. Cambridge and London: Macmillan, 1886.

Index of Scripture